AMATEUR DRAMA
production and
management

Martyn Hepworth

B T Batsford Limited *London*

In memory of my Father LYNE HEPWORTH
whose early encouragement showed me the
pleasure of amateur drama as a hobby

© Martyn Hepworth 1978

First published 1978
ISBN 0 7134 0937 1

Typeset by Tek-Art Limited, London SE20
Printed in Great Britain by
Billing & Sons Limited, London, Guildford
and Worcester
for the publishers
B T Batsford Limited
4 Fitzhardinge Street
London W1H 0AH

Contents

Contents

Contents

Preface

Hundreds of thousands of people in this country take part in amateur drama. For some it is a transient pastime but for many it constitutes their main leisure activity. Nearly all such people belong to amateur dramatic societies and it is with the organisation and running of such societies that this book is primarily concerned.

Amateur dramatic societies differ widely in nature, structure and size. They range from the large, powerful and successful to the almost unbelievably small. To pretend that the same problems are common to all, irrespective of size and resources, would be ridiculous and in reading these pages the reader is invited to adapt freely the solutions given to the situation in which his own society finds itself. An attempt has been made to deal primarily with problems, which in one way or another, are reasonably common to all societies but local conditions and traditions will always affect the validity of the answers.

The book makes no claim to original thinking. I have made an attempt to analyse problems and then to suggest lines upon which they might be resolved. Such suggested solutions are based on my own practical experience of running amateur dramatic societies for over twenty years, and at least it can be claimed that all the suggestions which are made, have been tested and found to work in practice.

In formulating these suggestions, I have been heavily dependent upon the experience of others, who, through the years have passed on to me the benefit of their knowledge and experience. In this connection, I would like to express my gratitude to the late Edward Plummer, the late John Prudhoe, the late David Maitland, and to Mr Colin Charlton and Mrs Mary Vincent Smith without whose help, over many years I

Preface

would not have accumulated that small amount of knowledge which has made the writing of this book possible.

Finally I would like to record my debt of gratitude to my wife, whose very considerable dramatic talents have been somewhat restricted in recent years by the more important task of raising a family, and whose helpful suggestions throughout the writing of this book have added immeasurably to its usefulness. It is true to say that without her invaluable help, a readable book would never have emerged.

Tunbridge Wells 1978   MARTYN HEPWORTH

Introduction

The amateur theatre in this country is far more than groups of people whose hobby is acting. Certainly the aspect of enjoyment is of considerable importance. No one would disagree that people who have a hobby should enjoy the practice of it. But the social implications go beyond the pleasure of those taking part. In an age when there is little touring theatre; when the professional theatre is mainly concentrated in the larger towns and the ability of the public to see drama of any kind is mainly confined to the television set, the amateur theatre movement provides an essential cultural link in the community which that community would be infinitely poorer without.

It is hardly accidental that amateur theatre is enjoying a renaissance at the present time; not only in the number of participants but, far more important, in the standards achieved. Standards which would have been thought acceptable 'for amateurs' only twenty years ago, would now be, and rightly, considered inadequate. In order to draw its public away from the television set in the evening, amateur companies have had to accept higher standards and maintain them. The fittest and best have survived and have adapted to this new situation. Concurrently, a resurgence of interest by the public in the live theatre has led to the successful establishment of theatre clubs in many towns which are too small to support a regular professional company.

The amateur theatre now is larger, better and healthier than it has ever been. It is not in any way in competition with the professional theatre. Indeed the two can be considered as complementary. A successful amateur company, consistently putting on plays of a high standard can attract a stable theatrical public over a period of time, and this public will support the professional theatre when it visits the district. Thus by keeping up high standards, the amateur theatre can open up areas for the reception of professional theatre which would not otherwise have existed and in so doing, help in the spread of good professional theatre away from those great centres of population where it is at present concentrated.

If the amateur theatre is to play the wider role in society which has been outlined and, at the same time, be fair to its members, then the society which sponsors it must be efficiently run. There is no longer any room for the kind of shoddy standards of organisation and management which once existed. If the amateur theatre is taking money from the public it must feel obliged to give the public its money's worth and the public themselves, rightly, demand it. Also in an age when costs are rising so rapidly, a badly run society can not remain in existence because it will be unable to pay its way.

The pages which follow attempt to give some guidelines to those engaged in running amateur dramatic societies today. The advice given is based on practical experience and everything that is suggested has been tried out, tested and found to work. It must always be remembered, however, that the advice given must be read against the background of local conditions and tempered and adjusted to fit local circumstances. Most dramatic societies have the same sort of problems and those problems are very often the results of lack of communication, lack of proper administration and lack of attention to detail. These factors combine to create far more work than there ought to be.

This book is not written merely for the benefit of ill-organised dramatic societies for, naturally enough, no dramatic society is really willing to admit that it is ill-organised. It is based on the assumption that in all dramatic societies, however small or however large; however wealthy or however poverty-stricken, there is always room for improvement in some area. When that area has been identified, then the society in question has come a long way towards improving it for itself. In suggesting solutions to specimen problems, this book is endeavouring to provide a measuring stick for societies to use, in order to identify the nature of their own problems and through this identification, seek their own solutions.

Introduction

Success in the amateur theatre is an elusive quality. It is not only to be measured by the size of the audience and its reception of the play; not only by the profits made and not only by the artistic excellence achieved. All these factors are necessary to each other and complementary to each other. Perhaps, speaking cynically, the best definition of success is survival.

An all-important aspect of success in the running of any amateur dramatic society is directly related to the degree of enjoyment derived by its members in their participation. People join dramatic societies to enjoy their hobby and to enjoy the company of other people of like interests. However efficiently a society is run, it will still fail unless its members enjoy themselves. If this appears to be ignored in the pages which follow, it is because the member's enjoyment is a direct reflection of the personality of the leaders of the society and it is not therefore an aspect which can be identified and discussed. If, in consequence, it is taken for granted here, it must never be taken for granted by those running a society. It is the factor which makes possible those benefits which are discussed later.

1 Committees and management

Differing forms of management

Not all amateur dramatic societies are run by committees. Many are run most successfully by a single individual on a paternalistic and sometimes almost feudal basis. Sometimes a producer, or simply someone who has organising ability and an interest in the theatre, gathers around him a group of people who have acting talent and, as a result of their united efforts, a show comes into being. There is no reason to suppose that this show will be any better or any worse than one which has been organised by a number of interlocking sub-committees, nor that the participants have been in any way cheated by not being asked to be secretary, treasurer, or committee member. On the contrary, many people greatly prefer to have their acting organised for them without responsibility. They have confidence in the individual who is organising it and, even if they do not, there is nothing to compel them to accept the invitation to take part. Having accepted the part, it is to be presumed that they are content to abide by the established customs of the group of which they then form a part.

It is necessary to make this point at the outset, since most of this book will concern itself with situations which assume a conventional society structure and the problems and opportunities which present themselves in that situation. There is nothing wrong with a group of players who are organised by a single individual, in which the individual players have no rights, as such, but the problems which it is the business of this book to examine, do not, in this instance, arise. Any problems which do arise will either be sorted out centrally by the organiser, or else the group will disintegrate and cease producing plays; its members will disperse to other groups either of a similar nature, or more conventionally organised. The fact that, for instance, society structure will be discussed does not mean to imply that this is necessarily being advocated as the best situation for all acting groups and organisations, simply that a large majority of groups do form themselves into societies, and, that having done so, experience certain problems which can be identified.

Beginnings

Nearly all dramatic societies, big or small, trace their origins to a small group of friends interested in acting, who got together and decided to put on a play. They do this either because there is no dramatic society of any kind in their area which they can join or because, for one reason or another, they are dissatisfied with the opportunities which are presented by those which do exist. In the first few shows that they jointly present and which are successful and enjoyable, there is generally no organisation of any kind. Everybody takes a share in doing everything and the impact of the natural initial keenness which brought the group into existence carries them through. Sooner or later, however, if the group is to continue to put on shows, some sort of policy will evolve and the individuals involved will find themselves repeatedly doing certain jobs in connection with a production either because they are good at them or because they enjoy doing them. At this stage the group will probably feel the need to give itself some sort of stability or permanence by becoming a society in a more specific sense of the word. Alternatively, it will take the joint decision to remain small, select, and directly member-controlled, taking all necessary decisions corporately. Either way, they will have taken a decision about their future and the group of friends will have become a society or organisation.

The act of becoming a society may be a deliberate decision which is taken or it may just happen. On the whole it is better if it just happens. If too much formalism is injected in the initial stages, there is a real danger that wrong decisions will be taken which will either stunt the natural growth of the society or even drive it out of existence altogether. If, for example,

immediately after that first successful show, a large committee
is formed and a constitution drafted, it will almost certainly
be based on someone's recollection of the constitution of
another society elsewhere and may be quite unsuitable for the
new group. There can be no standard constitution or society
structure for amateur dramatic societies everywhere. Local
influences and personal requirements, as well as individual
tradition, dictate that any structure or rule book must be
purpose-made. If reference is made in these pages to offices
such as publicity manager, for example, it is not to be taken
as implying that every society should have a publicity manager,
only that most societies do have an officer who bears a title
similar to that or an individual who does the work which that
name implies.

The growing need for organisation

If organisation of some kind is felt necessary in order to give
permanence to the dramatic endeavours of a group after an
initial successful production, then it should be of the vaguest
kind initially, leaving plenty of room for a more permanent
and lasting structure to evolve. A constitution, it follows,
which will tie the hands of the committee and the society is,
at this early stage, almost certainly a bad thing. An informal
meeting of interested individuals who, on the basis of one man
one vote, elect a chairman, secretary and treasurer and perhaps
three general committee members, is usually enough to bring
a society successfully into existence. Further needs can not,
at this stage, be accurately anticipated.

This newly formed committee will then probably take the
society through three or four more shows and, if they are
successful, fresh needs and fresh spheres of responsibility will
make themselves evident. Perhaps it will become apparent that
it is necessary to have someone in charge of the backstage
functions at productions on a reasonably permanent basis;
perhaps too, someone to handle the publicity for the society's
productions will be thought desirable. The success of the
society's ventures may have attracted a considerable number
of applicants for membership and it may be thought necessary
to have one member of the committee to look after the mem-

bers' needs and to preserve communication with them. Thus, from the vague beginning a committee structure is evolving which is tailor-made to the activities of the club in question and has not been rigidly imposed upon an unformed society into which it has been required to squeeze itself. The office should be created to fill a need and not the other way round.

It is thus evident that each dramatic society, by reason of its different birth and childhood, grows into a different individual with different needs, a different temperament and a different way of running its life. But just as we need two arms, two legs, a mouth, eyes and ears, for the body to function efficiently, so each dramatic society when it develops beyond the formative stage usually finds a need for officers to fill certain specific posts and to perform specific duties. Thus, normally a structure will evolve which consists of a chairman, secretary, treasurer, stage manager, wardrobe mistress, publicity manager, membership secretary and frequently also a number of committee members without specific responsibility. It is also generally found convenient to set a term on the length of time which these individuals can hold office without re-election by the members. So it will become customary to hold general meetings, usually once a year for the dual purpose of electing the officers for the ensuing twelve months and of hearing the views of the membership on the success or otherwise of the officers of the previous year.

Constitutions

Sooner or later, as the membership grows, the initial situation in which everyone was delighted with what everyone else was doing will disappear. This does not mean that beyond a certain period, dissatisfaction will be widespread. It simply means that it would be strange if genuine and reasonable differences of opinion did not begin to show themselves. At this stage it will become necessary to have some sort of rule book or constitution, initially so that the annual general meetings be run with some degree of consistency and so that the powers of the officers can be defined and regulated. Once it is understood, by a majority decision, in what manner the society is to be run and by whom, then dissidents have the clear option of either changing the rules, or the officers, or both, or of leaving the society.

It should not be supposed that the initial rule book, which will probably be little more than a code of conduct and a statement of intention, has the same sort of authority as the Laws of the Medes and the Persians. It will become necessary to change it as new needs evolve and no society should be afraid of doing so. If a change becomes necessary, the annual general meeting is usually considered to be the proper place to make it. Most people would consider that to give the committee the power to amend the constitution at will would be putting too much power in the hands of too few. It is also usual to specify that the constitution can only be amended if the proposed amendment is notified to all members in advance and if it is carried at the meeting by a two-thirds majority of those present and voting. This is usually considered to be a sufficient safeguard against wanton amendment.

This rather loose constitution should last for several years, during which time the society will either have gone quietly out of existence or else established itself as an integral part of the local scene. If the latter is the case, then it will probably be time to impose a more rigid and definitive constitution upon the society, since by this time its needs and priorities should have made themselves apparent. There is no set method of formulating a constitution since the needs vary to such an extent but any law-givers should bear certain points in mind. First of all, the power of the committee to make decisions on behalf of the club should be clearly defined and regulated. There is always a danger that a committee may feel that it can do exactly what it likes without reference to the declared policy and long-term aims of the club.

The rights of ordinary members to influence policy at a general meeting should be clearly defined in any constitution. The constitution should also make it clear by what method the shows will be cast, ie whether by audition process or not. If auditions are to be used, then the constitution should lay down clear guide-lines for audition committees. Lastly, the constitution should define the duties of the various club officers, taking care to be specific about their spheres of responsibility.

With this kind of constitution, tailored to suit the needs and preferences of the society in question there is no reason why it should not function happily and well for many years, but in case of future dispute or the presence of barrack room lawyers, it is always a sensible plan to have the draft constitution vetted by a qualified solicitor before putting it to the membership for formal acceptance.

The powers of the committee

Though the responsibilities of the committee will vary from club to club, as defined by the constitution, it can be said in general terms that a committee should concern itself mainly with the short and medium term policy of the club. It can perhaps be assumed that the long-term policy will have been established by debate at a general meeting of the members. Indeed, anything which seems to be a really long-term committment should be put to the members at a general meeting specially convened if necessary. The committee ought not to spend its time at its meetings discussing the relative prices of material for costumes and other minutae: this is the proper province of the officers in question who should bring their recommendations before the committee for approval or otherwise. It also seems pointless for committees to concern themselves with approving individually each single invoice that is submitted. They should approve a budget, and, provided that the expenses are in accordance with that budget, their payment should be left to the treasurer. It is very noticeable that committees which do concern themselves with these small details hold extremely long meetings and policy, which is the proper province of the committee, is almost entirely neglected.

It is certainly proper that the committee should concern itself with financial control. It is, after all, the custodian of the society's money for its year of office and it is to be expected that it will account properly for its stewardship at the annual general meeting. It must decide the policy of finance towards individual shows — whether or not a profit is to be expected and if so how much: it must control the expenditure of surplus funds if there are any and be prepared to show that it has spent them wisely and in the society's best interests.

Above all, a committee must decide what it wants to do and

not drift aimlessly from one show to the next, treating each production as an entirely isolated affair. This particular theme will be repeated again and again. In the pages which follow, the necessity of planning shows well in advance and of integrating the policy towards them will be stressed repeatedly. In this way a committee, unfettered by detail will be able to get on with its proper function — that of co-ordinating the policy of the society in a consistent manner.

Finally, any society should always be on its guard against committing itself too strongly to the committee principle. Though there may well be a case for sub-committees in some instances (particularly *ad hoc* ones to examine a specific project and report back), they are generally unnecessary and often have the result of preventing any real work from being done. The principle should always be that policy is best determined by a group; action is always best taken by an individual. Too many societies, in an effort to share the workload resolve themselves into innumerable sub-committees, all taking minutes, and all creating little pseudo-independent power groups. It is not at all surprising that under such circumstances it is often difficult to see the wood for the trees, and valuable time is spent at committee and sub-committee meetings which could be more profitably spent in actually getting on with the job.

With that cautionary word it will now be assumed that the society under discussion is being run by a committee, as most are, and that that committee has a genuine desire to work efficiently to create a happy and active society for its members and to be a faithful reflection of what its members want.

2 Choosing the play

Different methods of choice

Whatever their differences in structure and management, amateur dramatic societies exist for one reason only: that of putting on plays. All other aspects of their activities are subsidiary to this. It follows that the act of choosing the play that is to be performed is one of the most important things which any committee has to do during its term of office. Although some societies do as many as twelve productions a year, the vast majority do only two or three at most and thus for them, the play chosen represents the axis of the Society's activity for quite a long period. It is obviously important that the right choice is made.

Societies approach the making of this choice in a number of different ways. Some look for a play which is worth while doing as a piece of theatre; others, with a keener eye to the box office, look for something which the public will enjoy. Some look for a play which has a high female cast element while others look for one which has a large number of non-speaking parts so as to embrace as much of the membership as possible. Some committees have even been known to have chosen a play which presented good acting parts for themselves! None of these categories is necessarily exclusive and, of course, they do not represent a complete list of all the reasons for selecting a particular show. They are simply intended to show that choice of play can be governed by a wide variety of motives.

Differences in approach are identified with the time at which the producer appears on the scene; before or after the play to be performed is actually selected. Some societies prefer to make the choice of play and then look around for a producer (or competing producers) whom they will appoint to produce it. Other societies nominate the producer of their next show and then with him in mind choose what show it will be. In between these two extremes, a third method is to invite applications by producers to produce a play of their choice and then from the applications submitted, to choose both the play and the producer at the same time.

Choosing a play and then inviting producers to queue up to produce it (the first named method) is a luxury which only a very large and powerful society can afford. Producers are seldom two a penny and amateur ones will almost always want to have some sort of say in what play it is that they will be directing. Only if producing for a society is considered to be such an honour that a potential producer will be glad to produce any play within reason, will such a situation work at all. If a society lacking the necessary power, influence and prestige tries it, it will probably end up with no applications from producers. The second method (that of appointing a producer first) is far more common and, with smaller societies far more practicable. Appointing a producer first ensures that provided that a play can be decided upon which the producer likes and the committee approves, then the show will take place. In practice, of course, a producer accepting a society's general invitation to produce will instantly come forward with the name of a show which he wishes to direct or he may even present the committee with a list of plays which he would be willing to produce and invite them to select which they prefer.

With the medium-sized society, where there are probably two or more potential producers waiting in the wings, the third method (that of inviting applications) is probably most common. Even here it is possible for the producer who applies, to present the committee with a number of shows from which to make its choice and, certainly, the chance of making a mistake by this method is less than in either of the other two. It is not always possible to operate this third method, but when it is possible, particularly in the case of societies which pride themselves on their democratic approach, then it is generally the most acceptable. It has, after all, the very strong advantage of opening the production field to new applicants whose work may be unknown to the committee and who would therefore stand no chance by the second method. The committee does not have to choose them, but at least they have the chance of being considered. It is certainly the fairest way both to the aspiring producers and to the committee in vindicating its judgement at a later date.

Choosing the producer

Whether or not a producer should be asked to submit a choice of shows or just one is open to argument. Naturally, choosing between a number of shows, all of which the producer has indicated his willingness to direct, will be a more interesting task for the committee. It is not, however, as certain that the resultant artistic standard will be as high as if only one show was in question. Most producers will have one play which, at any given moment, and in the knowledge of the availability of certain actors, they really wish to produce. If forced by the terms of reference to submit others on which they are not so keen they will generally either submit plays which they will find easy to produce (perhaps ones which they have produced elsewhere) but to which they will not necessarily give as much enthusiasm and drive; or, plays which they think will sway the committee in its selection and this will also not always lead to the best dramatic performance. Personally I favour the application of the third method of producer selection, where possible, inviting applications on the one producer one play basis. At least this way it is reasonable to require the members of the committee to read the plays under review before making their selection as opposed to asking them to base that selection on a sometimes misleading synopsis.

Actually, the whole business of producer selection is generally much more straightforward than it has here been represented. In innumerable societies, one producer only is available at any one time and he or she is only prepared to produce one play. A take-it-or-leave-it situation therefore obtains. This does not by any means necessarily lead to bad results and many societies function happily and successfully on this basis for years. It is only dangerous if a society, happy in the competence and success of its resident producer, makes no effort at all to find and train successors. If they do not then the continued existence of the society will depend on the willingness of the producer 'father-figure' to continue.

New producers

Having said that a society should make an effort to find and train new producers, it is appreciated that this is a most difficult task. After all, a keen young actor can be encouraged and brought on by being given parts of increasing size and responsibility in successive productions, but this is not possible where a producer is concerned. For all producers there has to be the very first show that they produce, in which they have to assume the full responsibility that a producer bears. Naturally the risk is smaller if the individual producing for the first time is an actor or actress of long experience, who has watched others work, and who understands stage-craft thoroughly. But in order to have acquired this experience, they will often be middle-aged before they start producing and it is possible (though by no means certain) that their productions will tend to be derivative. Conversely, a society entrusting a production to a new and untried youngster, however keen, is taking a considerable risk. After all, the paying theatre public are entitled to expect a certain standard for their money, and the committee has got to be prepared to underwrite this standard in its appointment of a producer.

Societies which are really conscious of the need to foster young producing talent, generally do so in one of two ways, sometimes both. They hold workshop evenings at which improvised drama is encouraged and at which prospective young producers have the opportunity of producing small 'scenes' or 'incidents' with an improvised script. Provided that these are held regularly and carefully watched and organised they can not only be of great assistance to the young producer in finding his feet but also provide the committee with an excellent insight into the skill and inventiveness of the young producer in question. They are also valuable in providing an activity, which has a dramatic basis, to keep the club together between shows. Perhaps more obviously practical from the committee's point of view is to sponsor a series of club productions during the off-season at which literally anyone may have an opportunity of producing provided that they can find a cast. Although mistakes will obviously be made, these will provide a wonderful opportunity for the young producer to find out (possibly at first through the medium of a one-act or short play) what putting a production together is actually all about. The committee too, will be able to distinguish by this method between real ability which requires further encouragement and ill-advised over-enthusiasm which needs tactful deflating.

Popularity of the play selected

The selection of a producer and the selection of a play are so closely tied up that it is almost impossible to separate them. Indeed, as has been pointed out, with some societies they amount to exactly the same thing. But whether they are the same thing or not, the committee must make sure that the play chosen is one which the producer really wants to produce for only then will he or she do it well. There is less cause for concern on this point if a one producer/one show method of selection has been employed but if the play has been chosen first or if the producer has selected a number of plays, then it is a point which has to be watched. In amateur companies the enthusiasm as well as the technical competence of the producer is of critical significance and it is essential to be sure that this enthusiasm is genuinely present. A producer who is over-used may exhibit a declining degree of enthusiasm as the years go by.

Quite as important as the enthusiasm of the producer for the play chosen is the popularity of that play with the members. Of course a committee must retain the power to decide on what show will be performed, since it is its business to weigh the various factors which are involved and to come to a balanced judgement. The alternative — to select a play by popular vote at a general meeting — is frequently a recipe for disaster. Nevertheless it is necessary for the success of the production that the members of the society who will be acting in it, working behind the scenes, and selling it to the public, feel excited about the prospect of performing in it. If they do not then the auditions will be poorly attended and the necessary work in connection with the production will lack willing helpers.

The reception of the play chosen by the society as a whole

will show itself in a number of ways. A strong backstage team will look for opportunities in this department; a keen wardrobe mistress will probably prefer a costume play and an enthusiastic publicity manager will welcome one which will obviously be popular with the public. The point could be developed by example almost indefinitely but sufficient has been said to indicate that the committee must be conscious in its choice that it will have to 'sell' that choice to the membership.

Availability of cast

Apart from these personal and sometimes emotive factors which may influence a committee when it comes to deciding on what the next show will be, there are other factors to be considered. First, and most obviously, there is the question of cast availability. The play chosen must be one which the acting resources of the club can manage. This does not mean choosing a play which will provide a good vehicle for so and so, but that the committee satisfies itself that sufficient people are available for the play to be adequately cast. However enthusiastic the producer, or excited the club may be, the show will be a disaster if the actors are inadequate.

Technical considerations

Secondly the committee must look at the question of theatre suitability. This is not such an obvious factor as it may seem. Many plays which at first glance seem suitable may be ruled out after close examination. Some plays, for instance, in which a change of set is essential, which are easy to cast and which the producer likes, may have to be rejected because there is insufficient wing space to make the changes. Even if it is decided that by designing a composite set these difficulties can be overcome, the play may still have to be ruled out because such a set could not be adequately lit. Here the consideration of theatre suitability overlaps with that of technical possibility. Are the technical resources, both of men and equipment, that the club has at its disposal, adequate for essential technical requirements? If not, and if the requirements are really essential, then the play will have to be rejected.

Potential audience response

The last considerations are the potential audience response and the financial viability of the proposed show. Here the committee will be governed by its policy to productions in general far more than with the other considerations. For example, it may be able to take the attitude that it does not mind losing money on the show since it is such a worthwhile theatrical choice, or it may feel that although it will lose at least £50 on the show, it will make that up on a jumble sale. A show loses money either because the costs of production are too high or because the public does not come to see it, or both. An assessment of a show's financial viability is therefore directly related to its potential audience appeal. Committees differ greatly in their approach to this consideration. Some feel that they have a responsibility to put on a show which the village will want to come to, while others choose a show which they want to do and hope that they can sell it to the village. This difference in outlook and approach has relevance to the committee's choice of show.

One may well wonder how it is ever possible for all these differing and contrasting requirements to be met at one time, and the answer is, of course, that they can generally only be met in part and seldom in whole. The resultant choice of many hours of patient reading and discussion on the part of the committee will probably be a play which the producer is keen to produce; which a fair proportion of the members will like; which can probably be cast if certain people are available, or can be persuaded to be available; which is suitable for the theatre; which is technically possible provided that the producer revises some of his ideas; which ought to attract a fair audience response and which, if it does so, will just about break even. Under these circumstances the show is possible and the committee will have done its job in weighing carefully the important considerations that apply to any selection.

Choosing from an open field

Although the situation will be extremely rare, the committee may have a completely free hand to choose what play it will. It may be blessed with a society bulging with talent, a superbly equipped theatre and an established theatrical public. This situation is rare indeed, but it does sometimes happen, particularly with societies that own their own theatre. In this case the controlling consideration should be the preference of the selected producer. If the situation is even more Elysian and there are a number of producers available, all of whom can be called upon to direct a wide range of plays, then, strangely, the committee's task is even harder. Provided that the right homework is done, it is comparatively easy to choose between this play and that one; between this producer and that one but if the field is really open, where on earth do you begin?

In this extreme situation, or in the commoner variations of it, there is an opportunity for the committee to employ a dramatic policy. It will be able to decide that it wants to present a play of a certain type for the April date and then one of a very different nature for the June date and so on. The business of choosing a play need not be a matter of each member of the committee remembering one which he has seen and enjoyed in the past. The copyrights of a very large number of the plays which have been published are held by Samuel French, Ltd. This firm regularly produces a catalogue (or *Guide to Selecting Plays*) which, for ease of reference is divided into seven sections, each obtainable separately and each costing no more than 20p plus postage. The seven sections are: 1 Full Length Plays; 2 One Act Plays with Mixed Casts; 3 Plays for Women, 4 Plays for Men; 5 Full Length Plays for Children; 6 Religious Drama; 7 Revue Sketches. Every three months or so, French update this list by the publication of *Play Parade*, which is a list of the plays published by themselves since the publication of their last catalogue.* The information contained in these booklets is invaluable in guiding the committee in the selection of a play. The information contained (though necessarily brief) is sufficient to enable them to compile a short list of plays which co-

---

*Samuel Frency Ltd, also publish two other lists (obtainable free) which are of great value to any amateur society. *Books on Acting, the Theatre, Television and Opera* is a treasure house of useful books on the theatre in all its aspects, and is updated every three months or so in *Book Parade*. In addition, *Sounds Effective* gives a very extensive list of recorded sound effects that are obtainable. All these publications can be secured by writing to Samuel French Ltd, 26 Southampton Street, Strand, London, WC2E 7JE.

incides with their policy, and they should then send off for one copy of each. It is very well worth any society's while to pay the modest sum involved in becoming a regular recipient of this literature. Copies of classics are, of course, easily obtainable from any library. The plays selected should then be read by every member of the committee (no one is able to vote on a play that he has not read) and then, on the basis of discussion, the final selection made. Under no circumstances should the selection be made on the basis of the publisher's synopsis only. These, though generally well-written and not misleading, give no indication of the literary quality, of any technical difficulties which might arise in production, and, above all, how dated the dialogue.

Conclusion

The selection of the play for production (and of the producer to produce it) is one of the most important duties of any committee. It is also one of the most exacting but it should in no sense be skimped. It is the committee's responsibility to its members — not to mention the theatre-going public — to take infinite pains in making the right choice.

3 Casting

Methods of casting

To the average member there can be few aspects of his dramatic society's activity that are more important to him than casting. This is a natural priority. After all, most members will have joined for the chance to act, and since the opportunities to do so will be limited, the manner by which the plays are cast will be important.

It is likely, of course, that the choice of play and the choice of cast will, to a greater or lesser degree, overlap. No society, for instance, will decide to produce *Hamlet* without first being certain that there is at least one suitable and competent actor available to play the Prince of Denmark. Similarly, few prospective producers will submit shows that they would like to produce without being sure, in their own minds at least, that the show can be cast from the known resources that the society has at its disposal.

However, in discussing the question of casting, it is convenient to ignore the fact that 'pre-casting', whether official or otherwise, will have taken place and to approach the subject from the point of view of an open field.

As no two societies are exactly similar, either in structure or tradition, methods of casting will vary. They range from the ultra-democratic to the frankly dictatorial. The importance of the producer in the casting process varies from the negligible to the dominating, and generalisations are hard to make.

There is, however, at least one common factor, which exists only in the amateur theatre. When a professional production is being cast, the casting director will be governed in his choice by suitability and availability. In the amateur world there is also the question of fairness. Since amateurs act for pleasure, most societies consider it necessary to be fair to the potential cast in the allocation of parts. Such fairness must not, however, preclude the interests of the producer or the audience. A careful balance has to be struck and much of this chapter will concern itself with the ways and means of striking it.

There are two main methods of casting a play with innumerable variations within each of them. They divide at the existence or otherwise of an audition. Casting a play without an audition which will here be described for convenience as 'dictatorial' will generally take one of two main forms. Either casting will be in the hands of the producer alone or it will be done by a casting committee specially convened for the purpose or sitting for a number of shows.

The dictatorial method

The dictatorial method of casting is employed in innumerable societies around the country. Often, as with small, or village societies it is the only practicable method and frequently achieves excellent results. Fairness to the actor is largely ignored and fairness to the producer and to the audience is considered paramount. Where the supply of acting talent is limited, better results will usually be obtained in this way than by the use of more democratic methods.

This is not surprising. It is, after all, to be expected that a producer will cast his production from those actors and actresses who will do it most credit. Indeed it can be said that the extensive use of this system among smaller societies contributes greatly to the very high standard so often achieved.

With the dictatorial method, the producer or casting committee simply invites an actor or actress to play a part, presumably after having first discussed alternative candidates. The play then becomes very much a 'producer's play' — his choice of cast, his conception, his direction — and in this situation, the role of the producer is all-important.

Inevitably it lends itself to criticism and dissatisfaction. Members who disagree with the decisions or choice of the producer or committee, or who impute to them motives more sinister than straightforward, will feel aggrieved. It is natural that such dissatisfaction should be present, and in a few instances, of course, it is justified. Dissidents, however, should bear in mind that they presumably knew that this was the system when they joined the society and reflect that if the dissatisfaction is all that widespread, rules and traditions can always be changed. Often a dissatisfied minority forms a rival society of its own causing a fragmentation of the available dramatic talent, and so weakening the overall amateur standard.

✓ It is curious to note that these 'breakaway' groups often form rival societies which are identical in all respects to those which they have just left. The truth is, of course, that the protest of such dissidents is not against the system but against the application of that system in specific instances. They come to realise that although 'democracy' may be a convenient peg on which to hang their discontent, it is not always practicable.

The democratic method

In some instances, however, and perhaps in the majority, 'democracy' is practicable and when it is practicable it is generally desirable. Only by democratic methods can a society be seen to be fair to its members, and the way in which such fairness is made manifest is by the conduct of auditions.

Before passing to a discussion of auditions and their conduct, it is as well to add a few cautionary words. First, and most important, it should be appreciated that auditions assume an entirely different aspect according to which side of the audition table you sit. To those conducting auditions, the whole thing can be an interesting academic exercise; to those auditioning it is seldom other than a gruelling ordeal. For this reason it is important that auditions should have a relaxed and informal atmosphere, so that those auditioning can give as natural a performance as possible. If two rooms are available, it is often a good idea to organise a club social in the main room to help pass the time.

Secondly, those conducting auditions should realise that unless the audition passages are long and searching (which is seldom practicable) they can give only a valuable clue to the suitability of an actor for a part. Imagination must be used, as well as knowledge (if available) of the actor's past exper-

ience, before a casting is made. It is important that the choice
should be right first time and this is not always possible if the
game is played entirely by the book. Auditions can, and should
be, just as much of a test for those conducting them as for those
auditioning.

Most societies which cast by audition have either rules or
traditions which govern the conduct of the auditions. It makes
very little difference whether the audition is conducted before
the producer alone, before a specially appointed sub-committee
or a permanent auditions sub-committee; whether applicants
are heard individually or collectively. What is important is the
method by which the audition committee reaches its conclusions.

If a fair choice is to be made it is important that all members
are made aware in plenty of time of the date, time and place
of the proposed audition. If not all members know, then the
purpose of auditions defeats itself since not all members would
be given the same chance, and a situation could arise where
justice is seen to be done without actually being done.

If all members are notified of the audition, it must be
supposed that any who do not attend or who do not send apolo-
gies, do not wish to be considered for parts. On the face of it,
it seems hardly necessary to state this, but apprehension about
auditions, or even sheer laziness, sometimes means that members deliberately stay away hoping that the play will not be
fully cast and that they will be asked to fill a vacancy. For
them, the risk of not getting a part at all is preferable to the
terror of going to the audition. Such actors would really be
happier under a dictatorial system, where they would simply
be asked to appear.

Fairness and audition committees

The very fact that an audition takes place presupposes the fact
that fairness to the actor is regarded as of importance and the
question of the extent to which it should be a dominating
consideration naturally arises.

Although an audition committee is in existence because the
society wishes to be fair to its members, it must put this fairness
last in order of its priorities. First should come fairness to the

audience; then fairness to the producer; then fairness to the actor. It can happen that these priorities overlap or clash. If, for example, it is known that one applicant will give a brilliant performance but will be difficult to manage at rehearsal, then he should be given the part in preference to someone who would be easy to produce but who would give a less polished performance. Here fairness to the producer is taking second place to fairness to the audience. Similarly, if out of two applicants of equal ability one has a better record of punctuality and co-operation than the other, then he should be given the part — in this case, fairness to the producer being the dominating consideration. These very obvious examples have been given only to illustrate the central point which is that an audition committee, doing its job properly, will always consider its duty to the audience first; and that to its producer before its duty to an individual actor.

Within a very short period, an applicant at an audition has to demonstrate his potential to the maximum. In order to give him a reasonable opportunity of doing so, the form that the auditions take and, particularly, the audition passage which is chosen, are of considerable importance.

Opinion is divided as to whether auditions should be conducted with only the applicant in the room at the time or whether they should be group activities, even glorified play-readings. Personally, I favour the former method even though initially it may be slightly more nerve-racking for the applicant. But any producer or chairman of an audition committee ought to be able to make an applicant feel at ease, and a much more accurate result will be obtained if the temptation to copy other applicants, who have read previously, is removed.

Audition passages

Turning to the question of the audition passage itself, opinion is again divided. Some producers say that they prefer applicants to choose their own passage, sometimes not even considering it necessary for the passage to be taken from the play to be produced. Others would argue that such a diversity of readings can be most confusing if a balanced judgement is to be made and that, even more important, the element of contrast is removed.

It is certainly more usual for the producer to select, in advance of the auditions, passages from the play which applicants are then invited to prepare. Some even go to the extent of selecting a single passage for all male applicants and one for all females. Naturally this latter method makes it easier to strike a contrast, but on the other hand, it makes it more difficult for an applicant to prove to an audition committee that he is capable of playing a certain part, if the audition passage is not specifically related to that part. Much depends on the traditions of the society. If it is customary to audition for specific parts, then specific passages for those parts are perhaps to be preferred; if this is not customary then something is to be said for hearing the same passage from everyone. Few producers would feel that it is necessary to require applicants to learn the passage by heart, though some say it is more helpful to them.

Restrictions and limitations

I am conscious of the fact that when talking of applicants generally, I have referred to them universally as masculine. This is the customary usage in the interests of brevity but anyone who has had anything to do with auditions will, of course, realise that it represents, usually, the reverse of the truth. Audition committees may hear four or five women for each part and are lucky if they hear two men.

There are a number of reasons for this. Firstly, the majority of parts in most plays are for men. In Shakespeare, or in period theatre, this disparity is greatly enlarged and two or three women may be balanced in the cast list by twenty — or twenty-five men. Secondly, very few dramatic societies indeed have a membership which is at all equally balanced between the sexes. In most, female members outnumber males by something like two to one.

Some methods by which a society can compensate its female members for this disparity have already been discussed, but the disparity itself can have an effect on the outcome of auditions. Principal of these is that it is likely that the quality of the female cast will be higher than that of the male. Audition committees should start their work on the assumption that this will be the case and accept the disciplines which the situation imposes.

For instance, because there is likely to be a broader basis of choice, audition passages for the women should be longer and more searching. Even so, it is not always possible to cast the best female applicant. If women have to be 'paired' with men and there is only one possible male applicant, the casting of the female partner will be governed by the male casting and, consequently, the male should be cast first. This can sometimes mean that considerations such as height will govern the casting of the women whereas they will be irrelevant or of minor significance when casting the men.

With both the dictatorial and the democratic methods of casting, it is to be hoped that the same main considerations will apply. The main differences between them are in the extent to which the natural choice is circumscribed.

All audition committees will have their natural choice restricted to some extent. Some societies insist that everyone appearing in their plays must be members of their society. At the other end of the scale, some societies are content to allow a casting director infinite licence provided that lip service is paid to society membership.

Perhaps the most important restriction, and the most common, is the insistence on casting from those who actually attend auditions. The reluctance of society members to attend auditions has been mentioned and it has considerable relevance here, particularly if the tradition of the society is that applicants should audition for specific parts. The situation can easily arise where there is only one applicant for a certain part for which he is quite unsuited. Should he be cast or not? Duty to the audience obviously dictates that the best available actor must play, but auditions lose their point if the casting committee or producer simply award the parts without regard to those auditioning.

On the whole it is best not to tie the hands of the audition committee too tightly, or an unsatisfactory cast will almost certainly result. But while having few rules, it is good to have several strong traditions. Traditions can be changed or varied, whereas rules can not. In other words, to continue with the case of the solitary unsuitable applicant, a rule that a part must be cast from those actually auditioning for it would dictate that he was awarded the part and the show would suffer; a tradition that parts were awarded at audition unless there was a good reason to the contrary would mean that the audition committee could use its discretion if it felt strongly enough about it.

The embarrassment caused by a single unsuitable applicant is easier to avoid if a number of audition passages are selected which ALL applicants read irrespective of the parts for which they apply. Having heard all applicants read the same passage and noted their preference for parts, the audition committee can then distribute the parts on the basis of the reading as judiciously as possible.

Composition of audition committees

Three methods of democratic casting have been mentioned: that of the producer acting as sole member of the auditioning body; an audition committee specially convened for the production, and one which auditions all productions during the society year. Of these there is very little to separate the first from the dictatorial method. The only difference is that the producer goes through the motions of listening to applicants before announcing his cast. Democratic casting must imply the existence of a body of people making a corporate choice.

What then is the fairest way of assembling such a body? Qualifications would seem to be that it must be composed of society members who possess the ability to discriminate and who, for one reason or other, are not interested in appearing in the production themselves. The spectacle of an audition committee carving up the best parts amongst themselves (and this is by no means unknown) makes a complete mockery of the principle of democratic casting. Such restrictions may somewhat inhibit the choice of members for an audition committee but bearing in mind what has been said of the importance of auditions it will be clear that it is worth taking trouble over this choice.

Such qualifications come near to ruling out the committee which sits for an entire year because of the difficulty of finding competent members who are not interested in being in productions for a twelve-month period. This leaves the committee which is convened specially for a production.

In order to achieve a balance, it is useful if the producer is the chairman of the committee and that the committee itself consists of an even number (say four plus the chairman). This means that it is only necessary for the producer to have a casting vote, and avoids the charge that he is over-dominating.

It is always possible, and in some instances likely that all parts will not be cast at audition. To fill the vacancies there seems everything to be said for reverting to the dictatorial method. A series of subsequent auditions, concentrating on the vacant parts (often the least interesting ones) can be both unprofitable and frustrating. However democratically-minded a society may be, it can surely be argued that it has given its members every possible chance to apply for parts by announcing and holding auditions. If members do not attend, it should be assumed that they are not interested in appearing and the producer or committee should have a completely free hand in distributing such parts as remain at their discretion.

Putting mistakes right

It is entirely possible, particularly when untried or new members are considered at audition, that mistakes will be made. Mercifully this is not frequent but it does happen. Duty to the audience clearly makes it unthinkable that a producer should be forced to go through rehearsals with an actor who is obviously unsuitable, but, at the same time, it is an unpleasant task to have to tell someone that he is not going to make the grade. Often the situation sorts itself out. When an actor is really unsuitable for a part for which he has been cast, he is often as aware of it as those around him and a few well-chosen words can generally achieve an amicable parting.

When this convenient situation does not occur, however, there has to be a method whereby the producer can make the necessary adjustments. If the producer himself has cast the play then it seems entirely appropriate that he should tell the unsuitable actor of what has been, after all, his own mistake. If, however, the play has been cast by audition, then it seems only fair on the producer to supply him with a safety valve so that he is able to avoid the charge that he is wilfully disregarding the recommendations of the audition committee and is re-casting the show according to his own whim. In this case it seems best that a producer wishing to make a change in cast when rehearsals have commenced should be required to report this back to the committee who would themselves make the change after, if necessary, watching a rehearsal for themselves.

There is one exception to this. Very occasionally it will be necessary for a producer to make a change for disciplinary reasons. I was once present on an occasion when a senior member of a society turned up one hour late for rehearsal without an excuse, and extremely drunk. Rightly, the producer sacked him on the spot. Had he not done so it would have seriously undermined the producer's authority and rehearsal discipline would have suffered badly. Sacking a member for a reason such as this should be done only in the most exceptional cases, but when it is done it should be the producer's responsibility.

Considerable space has been devoted to the question of casting generally because, within an amateur group, it is a matter of the greatest importance. Most members of any dramatic society join in order to act and the method of casting controls their ability to do so. Furthermore the balancing of three 'fairnesses' — to actor, to producer and to audience — is a problem which is peculiar to amateur societies and probably the most difficult which they have to encounter.

Casting in departments other than acting

The casting of a production is not complete when actors and actresses have been allotted their parts. The success of an amateur show is dependent on the assembly of a good production team of which actors form an all-important part but only a part. Casting is completed when heads of staff have also been appointed: namely, stage director, wardrobe mistress, publicity officer, business manager and production secretary. Elsewhere the detailed functions of these officers will be examined: here we are only concerned with emphasising that they should be 'cast' at the same time as, or even before, the actors and actresses.

Highly organised or very large societies will, no doubt, have permanent officers (often specialists) to fill such posts. The vast majority of smaller societies will, however, appoint individuals to fill these positions for each new show. It is important that such appointments should be made quite as early as auditioning takes place, since it is possible that technical restrictions imposed by stage management or financial limitations may affect a producer's conception of the show and this, in turn, can affect the casting.

Only the heads of staff need be appointed thus early. These, together with the producer, constitute the production team. On the assumption that rehearsals will begin approximately one month after auditioning and casting are completed the production team should meet, at the latest, as soon as the auditions are over in order to plan the details of the production. Nothing is more frustrating for a producer than to start rehearsals without knowing the precise details of the set or the costumes. More important, a late start on the technical details will undoubtedly influence the artistic success of the production.

Any amateur production is overwhelmingly a matter of teamwork. Successful casting and a high standard of acting coupled with imaginative production can carry the show only a part of the way. It is necessary to lay emphasis on this, since too often it is the team aspect which amateur societies tend to ignore, feeling that the main problems are overcome as soon as the show has been satisfactorily cast. One has only to reflect on the 'humorous' and nearly always grossly unfair parodies of amateur drama in which stage hands wearing hobnail boots throw scenery about the stage, or the characters parade about in ill-fitting costumes, to see that in the public mind at least, the inadequacies of amateur theatre are largely concentrated on departments other than acting. Though such strictures seldom have the slightest basis in fact, it is undeniably true that attention to these details is frequently given too late for maximum effectiveness to be achieved.

In a like manner, the half-empty houses that are too often a feature of amateur productions, are frequently attributable to the publicity or business sides being tackled too late or too half-heartedly. Naturally, this is not always the case but too often blame is laid on other factors, such as unattractive or untheatrical surroundings influencing audiences adversely. Societies should be vigorously self-critical before they start blaming the public for lack of artistic appreciation. 'Selling' a show requires quite as much time and thoroughness as rehearsing it. Frequently the technical side requires even more.

Specific assistance and advice on problems concerned with a production other than acting will be given in subsequent chapters. The reason for introducing the subject into a chapter concerned with casting is to lay emphasis on the fact that casting the actors is only a part of the full casting process. As much care and attention should be bestowed upon the roles played by individuals in departments other than acting as upon the actors themselves. Only if the casting of all aspects is complete, thorough and successful, can the forthcoming production be viewed with the confidence that a paying public rightly requires.

4 Producers and rehearsals

Appointment of production secretary

When a play has been selected and cast (and even before it is cast) the chosen producer will need to consider carefully the way in which he wishes to organise his production; the extent and nature of the assistance that he will require to do so and, above all, his relationship with his cast as reflected in his management of rehearsals.

At the outset, the producer would do well to appoint a production secretary to work with him throughout rehearsals. The function of the production secretary is not a purely decorative one; nor is it one designed to give the producer added status. It is designed to fill the gap which exists between the professional theatre where the stage manager or theatre manager has certain administrative duties and the amateur theatre where, by tradition, they do not. Some channel of communication with actors outside the rehearsal room is always necessary and it is far better if, for example, the producer does not have to find time to address twenty envelopes or to make twenty phone calls advising the cast of an unavoidable rehearsal change. Of course, some producers do take on this function and all the many other things which fall within the administrative bracket, but if they do, it is possible that the quality of the production may suffer as a result. A producer should be concerned with acquiring the highest degree of artistic excellence that is possible from his production and unnecessary administrative duties will frequently prevent him from doing so.

In some societies it is accepted that the secretary undertakes these duties and attends all rehearsals in that capacity. In most societies of my experience, however, this is not the case and a special appointment has to be made for each show. The duties of a production secretary can be as many or as few as the producer chooses to delegate or as her own initiative leads her to assume. Like a good personal secretary in a commercial concern, she can become an unobtrusive, yet indispensable part of the organisation. It is not unreasonable, for example, for the wardrobe mistress to come to a rehearsal to check some measurements for costumes. Knowing the scheme of the rehearsal, and whom the producer needs and when, the production secretary can see that the wardrobe mistress gets what she wants rapidly and without interrupting the sequence of the rehearsal. She can always check what she has done with the producer, if necessary, at a more convenient moment. Anyone who has produced a show will know just how valuable this service can be.

The producer and the cast

Before rehearsals start, the producer should realise that he will face several problems which are entirely foreign to a professional producer. For instance, he is seldom in a position to dispense with a leading actor once that actor has been cast. This does not mean that a substitution can never be made (see Chapter 3) but it does mean that a producer lacks that ultimate control over his cast which a professional producer has. With this in mind, and while not diminishing his own authority, it is necessary for the producer to get the cast on his side at the outset so that their co-operation will be given willingly. There are a number of ways in which this can be done.

First by example. A producer's own enthusiasm for his production, even in those darkest moments which beset all shows, should know no bounds. He must always be at rehearsal well before the advertised time and assure himself that the set is made ready for a start at the time indicated. He must always give the impression that time is of value and see that it is utilised to the best advantage. As well as being friendly and good humoured, he must also exercise the authority which will make his direction respected. Above all he must consider the fact that time is important to his cast as well as to himself. Actors arriving for a rehearsal at — say — 7.45 in the evening, may have been home for only about three-quarters of an hour after a long and hard day's work; have had a hurried supper and experienced real difficulty in arriving on time. It will not be very popular if, when they have rushed to the rehearsal room and arrived to start at the advertised time, the producer changes his plans and keeps them waiting for an hour or more before asking them to do anything. Indeed I have sometimes known cases where actors have arrived at the start and not been used at all. I do not wish to imply that the actor's interest in the production is confined to a few brief moments during which he actually appears. The point is that the gap between the end of a working day and the normal start of a rehearsal is extemely short and the difference between asking an actor to rush to arrive by 7.30 or 7.45 and asking him to arrive at leisure by about 8.15, if it is known that he will not be used until then, will do more than anything to achieve a happy cast.

From the point of view of the producer, the importance of gaining and keeping the confidence and support of the cast can not be overstressed. Given that a producer is any good at all, then it must be assumed that the show will improve if the cast consents to do what he tells them. If they do so willingly and therefore at once, then valuable time is saved. The producer who resorts to bullying tactics will not only lose the loyalty of his cast and, having lost it will find it hard if not impossible to regain, but will also lose time since his instructions will be carried out, if they are carried out at all, under duress.

Planning rehearsals

The desirable situation of controlling a happy cast can usually be achieved if the producer plans his rehearsals carefully enough. He will know (or should know) roughly how much time he will need to rehearse each scene, act or sequence, how often he will need to do it and how soon he will want to start running the show in sequence. Having thought this out, he will know that if everything goes smoothly, a certain actor will not be required before a certain time. He should then publish this information in a rehearsal sheet, making this 'earliest time required' clear. In this way everyone knows where he stands and it also gives the producer much more reason to be firm if

---

SPECIMEN REHEARSAL SCHEDULE

Play: "The Merry Wives of Windsor"

Monday 10 May – Reading and discussion. Full cast at 8.00.

Thursday 13 May – Setting scenes 1-4.
Call at 7.45: Page, Mrs. Page, Anne, Mrs. Ford, Evans, Falstaff, Pistol, Bardolf, Nym, Shallow, Slender, Simple.
Call at 8.30: Host, Robin.
Call at 8.45: Caius, Mrs. Quickly, Rugby , Fenton.
Call at 9.00: Ford.

Monday 17 May – Setting scenes 5-8.
Call at 7.45: Ford, Mrs. Quickly, Falstaff, Robin, Bardolf, Pistol.
Call at 8.45: Page, Caius, Rugby, Host, Shallow, Slender.
Call at 9.00: Evans, Simple.
Call at 9.15: Mrs. Page.

Wednesday 19 May – Setting scenes 9-12.
Call at 7.45: Page, Mrs. Page, Ford, Mrs. Ford, Evans, Caius, Falstaff, Robin, John, Robert.
Call at 8.30: Anne, Mrs. Quickly, Fenton.
Call at 8.45: Bardolf.

Thursday 20 May – Setting scenes 13-17.
Call at 7.45: Page, Mrs. Page, Anne, Ford, Mrs. Ford, Evans, Caius, Mrs. Quickly, Falstaff, Shallow, Slender, John, Robert.
Call at 8.15: Host, Fenton, Simple.
Call at 8.45: Rest of cast except Robin.

Monday 24 May – Rehearse in sequence scenes 14, 1 and 8.
Call at 7.45: Anne, Mrs. Quickly, Shallow, Slender.
Call at 8.15: Page, Mrs. Page, Mrs. Ford, Evans, Falstaff, Bardolf, Pistol, Nym, Simple.
Call at 9.15: Ford, Caius, Rugby, Host, Robin.

Specimen rehearsal schedule which shows how a play with a large cast can be organised to give an even distribution of rehearsal time actors, even with these concessions, turn up late. It should be stressed that by calling actors for — say — 8.30, the producer is in no way committing himself to commencing their scene at 8.30; he is simply undertaking that he will not commence it before that time. Also it should be made clear that any actor is more than welcome to attend at the commencement of any rehearsal and indeed is encouraged to do so, but that he will not be 'late' if he does not turn up until the time shown on the rehearsal sheet. I have seen this method of rehearsal grow over the years with various societies with whom I have had associations and in all instances it has been an unqualified success. Producers not used to working in this way may feel that it restricts their scope, and of course their opinion is to be respected. No one would try to force any method of working on any producer. It can be shown, however, that those two evils which beset nearly all amateur societies at some time or another — lateness and absenteeism — have been massively reduced and in some instances completely eliminated where the producer has planned his rehearsals and thus tacitly acknowledged the fact that appearance in his show is not necessarily the very first thing in the lives of his cast.

When rehearsal sheets have been prepared, their distribution to members of the cast is the work of the production secretary and this should be done at a very early stage. If copies of the rehearsal sheets can be sent to all members before auditions, it is not at all unreasonable to ask members to declare at the auditions any rehearsals which they know they will be unable to attend and to mark in their diaries those nights when they are called. It is also part of the production secretary's job to note the arrival of actors and to advise the producer when he has a full complement to begin the first scheduled scene, at the same time reminding him of any known absentees for that evening.

Rehearsal atmosphere

Planned rehearsal will do more than anything else to establish that *rapport* between the producer and his cast which is essential for any artistic success. There are, however, other factors which can greatly assist. One is the atmosphere of the rehearsal room and its convenience and suitability for its purpose. Village halls, which are often used for rehearsals, are frequently ill-heated and underlit resulting in actors waiting to perform swathed in overcoats and scarves and hardly capable of giving of their best. Private houses which, by definition, have home comforts, seldom have rooms which are large enough for the adequate conduct of a rehearsal and the necessary untidiness that always attends a rehearsal in progress may well make the householder unwilling to offer the facility repeatedly. It is appreciated that frequently it is not possible to be discriminating in this matter — rehearsal rooms are often few and far between so that a society may have to put up with what it can get — but committees should treat the selection of a rehearsal room as high priority if they wish to give a producer and cast an opportunity of rehearsing a show to their full potential. They should not always seek the cheapest alternative, unless funds are so short as to make this essential. After all, the requirements of a good rehearsal room are fairly basic. It should be comfortably lit; adequately heated if the show is being rehearsed during the winter months and sufficiently large to be able to duplicate the area of the actual stage with sufficient room at the sides for spectators (actors not being used) to wait.

If these basic requirements in the rehearsal room are met, then there are a few other things that can be done with very little trouble, to make the general atmosphere more congenial. In most available halls it is possible to serve tea or coffee and if this service is offered, it does much to keep the cast happy while they are not occupied. Cost of the provision of this service can always be recovered by making a small charge per cup and there is no need to hold up the rehearsal while it is being served. Actors can simply go for their coffee when they are not required. Some societies go further and provide a mini-bar where alcoholic drinks are also available. Where these are being provided solely for the participants of the rehearsal (as opposed to forming part of an adjoining club-room) there are obvious dangers, and on the whole anyone who wants a drink will usually have time to get one after the rehearsal is over. There is, however, a case for alcohol if there is an adjoining room which can be used as a club-room and to which club members not participating in the production can be welcomed on rehearsal nights. The value of having regular club nights and their ability to foster an *esprit de corps* in the society as a whole, using rehearsal nights as a vehicle, go a long way to offsetting the disadvantages of having alcohol available on the premises. Such facilities must depend on the premises which are available for the society's use.

Duration of rehearsals

In discussing rehearsal planning, the period of time for rehearsal of two or two and a half hours has been indicated. Personally I consider this to be the ideal time but realise that many societies may consider it to be unnaturally short. Of course circumstances alter cases, and there may be societies whose members can continue to give of their best for periods of three or four hours on end. My own experience, however, is that with actors who have been working hard all day and then come to a planned rehearsal where, by definition, they will be much used, that there is a noticeable falling off of standard and effort after about two hours and that little is gained by continuing. Much of the advantage of a planned rehearsal will be thrown away if a producer, having got his cast together at set times, sends them away so late that they are getting over the rehearsal all the next day. As rehearsals near performance the tendency to allow them to grow longer is almost irresistible, as a sense of real urgency creeps into the proceedings. Yet this is the very time when it is most important to have the cast rested and well-prepared. With proper rehearsal planning and execution it should not be necessary for rehearsals to run late.

The prompt copy

In the work that he does before rehearsals commence, the making of the prompt copy is one of the most important jobs which a producer undertakes. The method by which this is done will be different with each individual producer. Each producer's method varies with his personality, the way in which he likes to work and the type of results that he wishes to achieve. No one can say that any method is right or wrong. They are just different. Some producers, for instance, will

IV i

Enter three witches
First Witch: Thrice the brinded cat hath mew'd
Second Witch: Thrice, and once the hedge-pig whin'd.
Third Witch: Harpier cries, 'tis time, 'tis time.
First Witch: Round about the cauldron go:
    In the poison'd entrails throw.
    Toad, that under cold stone,
    Days and nights has thirty one:
    Swelter's venom sleeping got,
    Boil thou first i' th' charmed pot.
All: Double, double, toil and trouble;
    Fire burn, and cauldron bubble.
Second Witch: Fillet of a fenny snake,
    In the cauldron boil and bake:
    Eye of newt, and toe of frog,
    Wool of bat, and tongue of dog:
    Adder's fork, and blind-worm's sting,
    Lizard's leg, and howlet's wing:
    For a charm of powerful trouble,
    Like a hell-broth, boil and bubble.
All: Double, double, toil and trouble;
    Fire burn, and cauldron bubble.
Third Witch: Scale of dragon, tooth of wolf,
    Witch's mummy, maw and gulf
    Of the ravin'd salt-sea shark:
    Root of hemlock, digg'd i' the dark:
    Liver of blaspheming Jew,
    Gall of goat, and slips of yew,
    Sliver'd in the moon's eclipse:
    Nose of Turk, and Tartar's lips:
    Finger of birth-strangled babe,
    Ditch deliver'd by a drab,
    Make the gruel thick, and slab.
    Add thereto a tiger's chaudron,
    For th' ingredients of our cauldron.

Specimen page from a prompt copy of Macbeth. *The facing page contains the producer's notes for his own reference. They are not detailed instructions*

Action	Effects	Lights
Around cauldron; 1st W, L; 2nd W, R; 3rd W, C	Thunder Slow kill thunder	Spots on cauldron Bring lights up
Rise and circle caul anticlockwise		
Resume first positions		
		Lightning
Circle clockwise	Flames from pot Thunder	
	Kill thunder	
Resume first positions		
		Lightning
3rd W rise 1st & 2nd W throw in alternate ingredients	Thunder Kill thunder	
1st W laughs		
3rd W squats		Lightning

sit down before rehearsals start and visualise and annotate every single move, pause and inflection which they will then painstakingly teach to the actors. Others, while having given some general thought to the overall concept of the show will arrive at the first rehearsal with a virgin copy and indulge in what — for want of a better expression — can be called instant direction. The validity of each method is complete; their practice, and that of the hundreds of variants in between depends entirely on the personality and requirements of the individual producer.

Whichever way a producer wishes to work — and it is his prerogative to choose — the existence of a fully marked prompt copy is essential. The only question is who marks it up and when. Presumably with the producer who pre-produces everything he will mark up a master copy before coming to rehearsals if only to remind him of what his own detailed thoughts were. In this instance it will only be necessary for the production secretary to have this copy (or a replica of it) before her and to mark in it any variations which evolve during the progress of rehearsals so that her copy then becomes a master which all other departments can use in assessing their basic requirements. Naturally her task will be far greater with an 'instant director' who may alter his mind frequently during rehearsal but, though the scale is different, the task remains the same. In the majority of cases the method of the producer will fall between these two extremes and so therefore will the task of the production secretary. In making this all-important master copy, it is certainly convenient if the production secretary can train herself to look out for the use of such things as properties and minor sound effects as the rehearsal proceeds and mark them (perhaps in a distinctive colour) in the master copy. This will mean that when property lists and sound plots etc., are required, the work of compiling them will be lessened. As with most other things, attention to detail in administration — in this instance the production of a full and accurate prompt copy — will save time rather than waste it.

The producer's overall involvement

The extent to which a producer should involve himself in

aspects of the production other than the actual directing of the rehearsals is a difficult question. The answer largely depends not only on the extent to which the society is already organised, but also what the custom of the society is in such matters. Although, I suppose, one of the messages of this book is that a society can be best organised by becoming efficiently and realistically departmentalised, it is only represented as the best way of ensuring continued success. In the ideal situation, stage directors, wardrobe mistresses and others will associate themselves intimately with a production from the word go; attending rehearsals and having frequent discussions. The producer will have no say, and indeed no direct interest in the sale of tickets or programmes. He just makes the show happen from the artistic side, and states what he needs for his purposes. Having said that however, I have been associated with some societies who have put on excellent shows, but which have had the invariable custom that the producer, once appointed, becomes a total dictator. He not only casts the show but also organises the publicity, instructs the stage staff in detail about the requirements and superintends the entire financial side of the production. However undesirable this may be in theory, there is no doubt at all that some producers prefer it and the artistic side of the production does not appear to suffer in any way from their acting in this manner. Obviously if it works, leave it alone. The most usual situation lies somewhere in between the two extremes which have been discussed above. Normally a producer will want to have a lot to say about design and construction of the set; will certainly want to lay down guidelines for costumes and properties and may also wish to express opinions and preferences about publicity and programmes. Certainly he will be in an ideal position, if he is willing, and able to do so, to act as a financial clearing house in conjunction with his production secretary. Provided that the artistic side of the production does not suffer through increasing the producer's involvement beyond actual directing, there is no reason why it should be discouraged. In very many instances it is the only way in which small societies can achieve a consistent theme in the work of their departments. For practical purposes a producer should be as much involved as he wants to be and as much as the society feels that he can be.

Maintaining impetus

Once rehearsals have started, there will always be an enthusiasm for the show (or if not there will be something very wrong indeed) which will sustain itself for the first two or three weeks. After this, there will be just as natural a falling-off in enthusiasm, when the real difficulties of the production become apparent. If the play is a comedy, the humour of the lines will cease to be as funny as they were when the play was initially read; if it is a drama, then the dramatic scenes will not yet be good enough to be really dramatic and will be in the stage of appearing 'ham'. This is a critical stage in the rehearsal sequence for any producer and the one at which his own mettle will be most severely tested. It is the time when he must inspire his cast to give of their best and to work hard. Some producers, of course, are able to do this through the strength of their own personality; their own popularity or their own ability to engage in repartee. They must come to terms, however, with the fact that this inevitable stage of disillusion will come and that they will have to cope with it in the best way that they can.

The best safeguard against disillusion is in trying to ensure that the cast enjoys the actual process of rehearsing. This is very much part of the producer's job. He should never forget that amateurs act in the first instance because they enjoy doing so or imagine that they will. When they cease to do so and cease to look forward to coming to rehearsals, their effectiveness as actors and the potential success of the show will be in jeopardy. It is just not good enough to take the view that they have said that they will do the part and that it is therefore their responsibility to see it through. They are not professionals; they have not contracted to work for the society for a wage. Honour and loyalty possibly, self-respect probably, will ensure that they will not let you down totally on the night, but this is not the way to achieve a successful production. It is therefore part of a producer's job to spot the appearance of this stage of disillusion and to take steps to remedy it. If he has sufficient authority or reputation to rely on himself to do so, all well and good, but if not, he can still do certain things which will help him. A social get-together with wives and friends at this stage in the rehearsals is often a good idea, as is the production at rehearsals of anything visual, such as a small painted model of the set or the design of the publicity or costumes. These will help revive the actors' interest and give them a new talking point. At this stage, unless the occasion is really outrageous, the producer should refrain from over-harsh criticism of the actors, and since this stage generally coincides with the time at which words should have been learned but are not, and the actors have developed a conscience about it, praise for those who have made a real effort with their words as opposed to strictures for those who have not will often have a worthwhile effect.

The successful producer will give close attention to controlling the impetus of rehearsals. Initially it will need to be restrained, since the greater the initial excitement, the stronger the disillusion; then, as has already been mentioned, the cast will need to be bolstered and encouraged. If both of these policies have been successfully carried out then when the third stage is reached, when the knowledge that the show is only three weeks away and that it is nowhere near ready for production, the producer should be in a position to give his cast the conviction that application during those three weeks will secure a result of which they can all be proud. Actors are seldom willing to admit that from the inside they really see very little of the game and that only someone watching, as it is a producer's job to do, can really tell just how good or bad a production is at any stage. Sustaining the rehearsal impetus is one of the most important functions of any producer since only he can recognise the stages and deal with them.

Conclusion

It has not been the intention of this chapter to provide a guide to producers. What we have been concerned in doing is identifying the function and role of a producer within the scope of an amateur dramatic society; defining the extent of his influence and power and indicating a number of problems and set-backs that are common to nearly every dramatic society in the country. The method of dealing with those problems will vary with the precise nature in which they present themselves and with the personality of the man or woman who bears the responsibility as producer for doing so. If he is not capable of doing so, then it will do the society no good to allow him to occupy the producer's chair.

5 Planning the Production

The people concerned

When a play has been chosen for production, all sections of an amateur dramatic society will need to concern themselves with the business of putting it together. The producer's feelings on settings, costumes, properties, special effects and sometimes publicity will need to be discovered. These requirements will then have to be worked out in detail by the stage director, the wardrobe mistress and others and the results of their workings will show whether the society can afford to put on the chosen show in the manner in which the producer wants or whether amendments will have to be made. Before examining the financial side of production planning, it will be well to take a closer look at the individuals who will be concerned. Although the planning itself will be done in a great variety of ways, in accordance with the traditions of the society, and in line with the personal preferences of the individuals concerned, it will be assumed here (for convenience only) that the requirements will be compared and the decisions taken by a production committee.

There is no ideal composition for this production committee and, depending on the society and the show which has been chosen, various individuals will be essential or superfluous. Usually, however, seven individuals are indispensable. These are: the producer, the treasurer, the stage director, the wardrobe mistress, the set designer, the publicity manager and the production secretary.

Most of these individuals, apart from the producer, whose role was discussed in the previous chapter, will have had groundwork to do before coming to the meeting. The treasurer will need to have briefed himself thoroughly on the general committee's policy towards the question of profit and loss; will have to have an up-to-date knowledge of the exact state of the society's finances and future requirements and, if possible, a knowledge of the box-office returns of previous shows of a similar nature. The stage director will have to have an accurate knowledge of the state of the society's store; the condition of the flats; the current price of timber and hardboard; what sound and lighting equipment is available and what key members of his backstage team will be available for the production. The wardrobe mistress (particularly if it is to be a costume play) will need to know the exact state of the costumes in the society's wardrobe; the approximate cost of replacement; the cost of making the sort of costumes likely to be required for the period in which the play is set and the availability of costume designers and seamstresses. The publicity manager will need to have made a detailed plan of the means by which he will publicise the show and obtained an exact costing of it. He may also be required to give a box-office return prediction, although this may be undertaken by the treasurer. The set designer will have had to produce rough sketches from which approximate estimates of costs of construction can be made and the production secretary will need to take notes on all the decisions taken. For much of this initial information, discussions with the producer will already have taken place. In particular, the wardrobe mistress will need to have discussed the type of costumes which the producer has in mind: the set designer will have had to agree with the producer the broad outlines of his designs as well as having discussed them in general terms with the stage director. Even the publicity manager may have discussed the type of publicity to be employed with the producer, particularly if the producer is publicity-conscious. The stage director, too, will have to have foreknowledge of any particularly difficult effects which the producer may have in mind and considers to be essential to the success of his production.

Achieving effects inexpensively

The object of these preliminary discussions is that a budget for the production, which bears some resemblance to reality, can be prepared. It will usually be known, even without discussion, whether the society is rich or poor and whether the production in question is likely to be expensive or otherwise. Few problems are likely to arise if the society has plenty of money and it is therefore likely that each department will be able to indulge its preferences. Similarly problems are likely to be few if the show can obviously be mounted on a shoe string budget or clearly will be a box-office winner. The problems will arise if the society has no money that it can afford to lose; if the proposed show is an ambitious one and the box-office receipts are likely to be uncertain.

This being the case it is as well to stress that ambitious productions can be mounted cheaply without losing any of their dramatic effect. It is necessary that set designers should understand this since it is in their department that the treasurer's axe is most likely to fall. It certainly does not follow that good set design is automatically expensive set design which requires extensive constructional work to achieve its effects. By far the most talented set designer for amateurs that I ever knew was also the simplest and the cheapest. His sets cost practically nothing but it was worth going to see the show just to see one of them. I shall never forget the way in which he designed the pastoral scene for *The Winter's Tale.* He achieved different levels by the use of rostra which were part of the standard equipment of the theatre. About twenty cleverly arranged bales of hay, two rustic tables, a long ladder, a farm cart and several earthenware bowls of colourful flowers made up the set which was played against a simply lit cyclorama. The effect was staggering and was greeted by prolonged audience applause, but all the items were borrowed and, apart from minimal expenses on transport, cost the society nothing. The talent of the set designer lies in his ingenuity to utilise the materials at his disposal to the maximum advantage.

The same principle applies to costuming the show. Later the technique of buying inexpensive materials to achieve maximum effect is dealt with in detail but it is worth recording here that I have seen many ambitious productions which have dispensed with period costume as such altogether. *Henry V* was once played to great effect by simply wearing differing (but well-

made) tabards over black polo-necked sweaters and jeans.
Faust was played in white open-necked shirts and black trousers
or skirts. This is not the same, of course, as setting the show
in modern dress, which is also an alternative. It is the technique
of using an unobtrusive costume or a uniform one which the
audience will accept a few minutes after the curtain rises or
else, as in the case of *Henry V*, in using pieces of material
and basic garments to suggest others.

Preparation by departments

There is thus much homework to be done by all the various
departments before any meeting to discuss the financial viability of the proposed plans can take place. In a well-run society,
such enquiries will be made automatically by the individuals
concerned who will realise that they will have to answer certain
questions at the production meeting and will wish to have the
answers ready. It perhaps needs to be emphasised again that
all these enquiries will take place long before rehearsals or
detailed planning of the production by the producer takes
place. The precise nature of the set, for example, will have to
be decided before the producer does any detailed planning at
all; so to a lesser degree will the details of the costumes and the
sound and lighting plots. For the producer to plan properly
it will be necessary for him to be furnished with a detailed
set plan, accurately drawn, on which he can plot the move-
ments. Nothing is more irritating to actors or frustrating to
producers than to have to change moves half-way through
rehearsals because of an amendment in set design.

Establishing the requirement

With the homework done, the all-important meeting of the
production committee can take place and the various departments can compare notes, under the watchful eye of the
treasurer. Although the purpose of the meeting is to prepare
and agree a budget for the production, the statement of the
requirement should precede it. Seldom does it work if it is done
the other way round. Although there is a risk that the production committee may spend more than necessary if a society

decides in advance what it can afford on a given production, this is remote. A much stronger argument in favour of the requirement coming first is that the whole process of production planning is greatly shortened, as has been shown, if the various departments prepare mini-budgets, however approximate, before the meeting. This advantage will be lost if the amount of money available is declared before anything is done. Societies which insist on putting the budget first generally do so by saying in advance that there is so much money available; that so much will be required for hire of hall; so much for rights; so much for incidental expenses; so much for publicity; leaving so much over for costumes, set and effects. A discussion between the stage director and the wardrobe mistress will then reveal how they can split up the available funds but it is rather like planning with a pistol pointed at your head.

If, as is most likely (with the requirement coming first) the total sum required by all departments is more than is available, or can be recovered through box-office receipts, then it is often a comparatively easy exercise to ask each department to economise by — say — 10 per cent, if this will achieve the required saving, or to notice where the really big spending is and to wield the axe there. Thus, in the opening stages of the production meeting, the difference between prospective income and expected expenditure will have been established and guide lines will thereby be given within which the committee can work without wasting too much time.

In presenting their mini-budget to the production committee, the various departments will have to be prepared to be as exact as is possible and their previous enquiries should have been detailed. The stage director, for example, will have to have attempted a costing on how many flats will have to be made or hired and what the cost of paint or other materials will be. He will have spoken to the producer about special lighting and sound effects which may incur expenditure or may be able to be achieved through owned or borrowed equipment. With these details at his disposal, he will be able to prepare a rough budget for his department to which, at this stage, he should add at least 20 per cent for contingency. The wardrobe mistress also will need to cost her own preliminary enquiries and to make the same allowances.

SPECIMEN BUDGET SHEET

Required expenditure		*Expected income*
Hire of Hall	70.00	Expected attendance of 800, based on average of last five shows.
Rights	42.00	
Administrative expenses	10.00	
Set construction	45.00	
Paint	15.00	Average seat price of 65p gives box office sales of £520 and profit of £86.
Special lighting	30.00	
Special effects	15.00	
Wardrobe	65.00	Average seat price of 55p gives box office sales of £440 and profit of £6.
Printed publicity	65.00	
Press advertising	35.00	
Direct mail	7.00	
Six sheets	5.00	Average seat price of 50p gives box office sales of £400 and loss of £34.
Sundries	10.00	
Contingency allowance	20.00	
Total expenditure	434.00	Expected programme sales £35.

Break even position is achieved by average seat price of 50p.

N.B. The above figures assume that the cost of production of the programme is exactly covered by the advertisement revenue.

Specimen budget sheet showing how to arrive at a suitable price for the seats by comparing possibilities with the required expenditure

The treasurer, having taken note of the individual requirements, will add extra-departmental expenses such as hire of hall for rehearsals and performances, rights, a provision for properties, administrative expenses and other customary items. To this will be added the amount required to publicise the show from the detailed costings given by the publicity manager, and the requirement has been established for putting on the show as the producer and the department heads would wish to see it done.

Achieving a balance

An assessment is then attempted of the income which is likely to be derived from various sources, principally, of course, the sale of tickets. It is important that this figure should be more exact than the opening figures for the expenditure on the production, since these can be covered against slight inaccuracies by the contingency allowance. The comparison of these two figures — the expected income and the required expenditure — will show whether the production as at present planned is likely to make a profit or a loss. Naturally, if a large loss reveals itself, cutting will have to take place and, of necessity, this will tend to confine itself to set, costume, effects and property requirements since it is unlikely that publicity can be cut without affecting the income and the society can hardly alter such charges as hire of hall and rights. If it becomes obvious that no amount of cutting will produce a balance, then there are three options open: to abandon the production because the society can not afford it; to request the committee to accept the inevitability of financial loss to a certain maximum; or to examine means by which the ticket sales can be bolstered by other methods in order to eliminate the deficit (see chapters 9 and 10).

In practice, the treasurer should invariably know what the policy of the committee is likely to be on any of the three options and the problem will usually be solved by cutting expenditure. Certainly, if the treasurer is doing his job well as a general committee member, he will have already established a policy towards the show in question: either that the committee will be prepared to accept a loss up to a certain figure; that it expects the show to pay for itself but does not expect a profit of any size to be made, or that it is looking for a target profit of so much. Only if the detailed costings show that it is quite impossible to conform to the committee's policy by cutting expenditure, will he need to report back. It is also likely that the various spending departments will see that their suggested requirements can be cut by a certain modest percentage and will be able to assure the treasurer of their ability to do this without at that stage giving definite details. Finally a precise budget will be agreed and accepted by the treasurer.

The process of arriving at a budget has been greatly simplified in the telling. In effect it will probably take several weeks for all the preliminary costings to take place, be rejected, reexamined and revised, and more than one meeting of the production committee will almost certainly be necessary. The result, however, will be the same. At any event, the discussions and meetings should take place well before the rehearsals commence and will take less time if the department heads are well briefed upon the resources of their various departments, and if the committee's policy towards productions has been clearly defined.

The role of the publicity manager

The publicity manager is a very important member of the production committee. His job is to estimate the box-office return (assuming that, as is usual, ticket sales are handled by his department) and to advise the treasurer or committee accordingly. He may also be in charge of the programme if it is considered as a source of revenue, and may even combine his duties with those of front of house manager and thus be in charge of the theatre bar. If this is so, then all means of income directly related to the show will come under his control and the ability of the production to pay for itself or otherwise will be largely in his hands. The detailed duties of the publicity manager are dealt with in Chapter 8: here it is only necessary to stress that publicity planning must commence very early indeed. While other members of the production committee must know their requirements only roughly, the publicity manager must know his in detail and in order to do so must have already formulated detailed plans.

The concern of the publicity manager with finance is not always understood. What has been said already will make it clear that the income for the show is really entirely in his hands, but he will only be successful if the expenditure, which is in the hands of others, is not exceeded. For this reason, some societies combine the posts of publicity manager and business manager; the function of a business manager in this context being to monitor expenditure during the course of preparation for a production. It is entirely arguable that a 'business manager' is just making another post out of part of the treasurer's job, and, to an extent, this is true. A treasurer can be as capable as anyone of fulfilling this function: it all depends on the policy

of the society. If the treasurer is very much part of the production team, there is none better to do this job. If, however, he
sees himself mainly as a book-keeper, and several treasurers do,
then someone is needed to fill this role. It can easily be the
publicity manager, or a member of his team. A business manager
will insist on detailed estimates for all requirements before
purchase, will insist that all bills are submitted to him for
approval and will rigidly control the spending of contingency
money. Any expenditure other than that specifically agreed
will have to have his approval and in this way he will be able
to keep a check on expenditure as preparation for the show
proceeds. Only if such a check is kept, and is known to be
being kept, either by himself or another, will the important
decisions of the production committee make any sense at all.

Assessing a production

The production committee should not go out of existence when
the curtain goes down on the first performance. Perhaps, at
that stage, the producer might be excused further participation,
but the rest have a job to do after the show is finished which is
almost as important as the job that they did before. Usually
when a show makes a large loss which was not expected, a
panicky committee holds several meetings to decide why the
catastrophe happened. It is just as important that this 'post
mortem' should be held for a show that has been highly successful. If you have lost a lot of money, no amount of talking
will bring it back, although you may be able to take measures
to ensure that the same mistakes are not made again. If, on the
other hand, you have made a lot of money, then by identifying
the successful formula and applying it on a future occasion,
you may be able to be equally successful next time. For either
of these conclusions to be correctly drawn, a detailed analysis
of the production must take place immediately it is over when
all the facts are fresh in everyone's minds.

Naturally, the right people to do the analysis are the production committee, for theirs was the task of agreeing the
financial allocations in the first place. Their task now is to find
out how accurate their calculations really were. If they were
accurate, then the method by which they were reached should

be preserved so that it can be used again in the future. If they were inaccurate, then the reasons why these inaccuracies occurred should be probed and adjusted so that once again evidence will exist of the mistakes made. The production committee for the next show, and even more for the next show but one will probably not consist of the same people as the one that has just finished and unless lessons can be handed on in some tangible form, then the same mistakes will be made in future.

While, in the post-show analysis, it is obviously important to scrutinise the expenditure side, the income side is no less important. Here, the analysis is not merely a case of identifying mistakes, but of making constructive suggestions for the guidance of future production committees. Such questions as: was everything done to bring in the maximum audience? was money lost through careless accounting in the administration of ticket bookings? was publicity overspent in relation to the results achieved? — should be asked and answered.

Conclusion

If the method of running a production is through a committee — as has been here assumed — then there are as many different ways of organising this committee as there are societies. The only wrong way of doing so is the way which does not achieve the desired results: the only right way is the way that works. Provided that the essential planning, execution and assessment is accurately done, then the society should employ the method that it finds easiest and most effective. It is in the cases where this essential work is not done at all, or is done inaccurately, that financial disaster befalls societies and problems arise which could otherwise have been prevented.

6 Building a backstage team

The attitude of a society

Most amateur societies will be aware of the value of good backstage arrangements, run by competent personnel. It is unnecessary to lay emphasis on a truth so self-evident. In this chapter
we shall examine the people who make up the backstage team,
define their functions, their status, and how other members
of the society can assist them in their different tasks. In the
next we shall look at the equipment used.

Strangely, although most societies readily acknowledge
the importance of backstage arrangements, few employ any
sort of central policy which, over a period of time, would lead
to the emergence of backstage specialists. Too often, societies
with funds which should enable them to make better arrangements, require their backstage staff to do the essential work of
preparing for a production in cold, inefficiently lit garages
with no workbench or proper facilities. Because the leaders
of the society are primarily motivated towards acting, they are
content to appoint a stage manager — itself a meaningless
term without the proper back-up staff — and leave him to make
all arrangements, contenting themselves with bemoaning the
lack of interest shown when these results are, predictably,
inadequate.

The man or woman who is interested in acting — in being in
a play — will naturally gravitate towards the amateur dramatic
society as the obvious field for the pursuance of their hobby.
The backstage specialist is a different animal. For him or her,
joining an amateur dramatic society, while it may be ideal, is
by no means obvious. It will not instantly occur to the boy
who is interested in carpentry or electricity, or to the girl

who is interested in dress design or dress-making, that an amateur dramatic society is an outlet for their talents and interests.
Yet they are the essential raw material upon which an efficient
backstage team is built, and, since they will not naturally come
to the society, the society must come to them.

If it is not acknowledged that the society itself must take the
initiative, it must not be supposed that a sudden burst of
enthusiasm will build a backstage team overnight. It is a process
which will probably take two or three years, and during the
whole of that time the society's impetus must be fully maintained. It is certainly a long-term committment, requiring
patience and dedication, but the results will be beyond price.

A backstage policy

If a society contemplates taking up a backstage policy, then
there are two essential preliminaries to any action. First, there
must be a senior officer of the society — presumably bearing
the title of stage director — who will oversee and organise the
emerging backstage team. It needs to be stressed that this
individual need not necessarily have a great deal of technical
knowledge — this is not his function — but he does need to be
a good organiser, and he does need to be committed. It will be
difficult, for example, for him adequately to supervise the
building of a backstage team if he himself is expending most
of his energies in rehearsing a part in the current production.
His first responsibility and the first call on his time must be to
his own staff and to representing their interests lucidly and
efficiently to the committee.

The second essential preliminary is that before any recruiting
is done, some sort of proper workshop and/or store which is
reasonably equipped must be provided. If the society in question frequently does costume plays, and a part of its backstage
policy is to build up a wardrobe stock, then a suitable store for
this must also be provided. Naturally, finance enters strongly
into the argument here. Renting a store and equipping it must
cost some money but provided that the money is there, it will
be well spent. If the money is not there, then it can perhaps
be raised by the various means open to a society and, as the
next chapter will show, can often be made a source of con-

tinuing income. However, unless a society is prepared to raise, and having raised, to spend the money on these items, it will not be able to pursue the kind of backstage policy.

The rooms which have been mentioned — the workshop, the stage store and the costume store — need not be lavishly appointed; their basic requirements are comparatively minimal. The workshop should be at least twelve feet square, should be dry, efficiently heated and lit — and clean. It should contain a workbench with a reasonably efficient vice. It should be easy of access so that a 10ft x 4ft* flat can be carried in and out without undue problems. The stage store has no basic requirements except that it should be free from penetrating damp which would result in the deterioration of the items stored there, and that it should be comparatively easy of access. The wardrobe store must also be dry and should contain rails on which costumes can be hung. These can be either made or bought second-hand from a store that is replacing its own.

None of these basic requirements is unduly expensive and the capital sum involved is therefore comparatively small, but they will make all the difference to the success of the society's policy. There remains the question of rent. This need not be high since the premises do not have to be in a prime position, nor does the period of lease have to be long-term since all the contents are readily moveable. Often local councils have sheds or warehouses that they own but which are empty because the property is ultimately scheduled for redevelopment. Diligent enquiries among Estate Agents will sometimes reveal property which it is anticipated will be empty for up to three years and which the owner would not mind having heated and maintained in the meantime for a comparatively nominal sum. I do not wish to suggest that the search for premises is ever easy; only that determined enquiry and ingenuity will generally reveal something. It all depends on how seriously the society regards the importance of the creation of its backstage team.

Recruitment of personnel

Having provided the necessary facilities and appointed a senior officer of the society to be in charge, the society is now ready

*See footnote on metric conversion on page 77.

to move into the second stage of its policy, which is to recruit the all-important personnel. In nearly all cases once the committee's interest in backstage facilities is known, existing members, or husbands or wives of existing members will come forward and either form the nucleus of a team or, indeed, the team itself. In this happy situation, there will be little for the stage director to do but mobilise his forces. A much commoner situation, however, is that a society which has neglected or ignored the contribution of its backstage staff for many years, and has just decided to employ a backstage policy finds (hardly surprisingly) that it has large gaps in essential departments, even taking into account the awakened interest of its existing members.

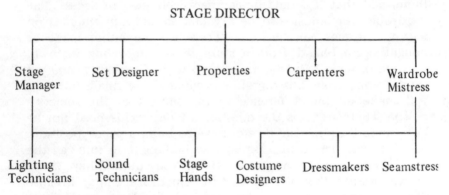

The backstage team

If this is the case, the society will need to recruit set designers, lighting technicians, carpenters etc., from scratch and the paragraphs which follow give some indication of the areas in which this recruiting can be profitable. It needs to be stressed however that this recruitment is very much a double-sided arrangement. The society is not just recruiting a lighting technician — for example — so that the next production will be better lit. Even more important, it is introducing the individual concerned to an area of activity, consistent with his talents, which he will find rewarding, interesting and enjoyable. If this is achieved, the recruitment will have been successful.

Naturally, the most effective backstage team, however uncommon it may actually be in practice, is a team of dedicated specialists who have not the slightest desire ever to appear on a stage in an acting role. There will, however, be very few societies indeed where this will be the case. In most, actors taking very small parts or other actor/members of the society who are not engaged in the current production, will find themselves filling in as temporary stage hands. For this reason, for the purposes of this discussion, it will be convenient to ignore the unskilled areas of stagecraft upon the slightly dubious assumption that a sufficient 'labour force' will be available, and to concentrate upon the skilled areas where new members may need to be attracted into the society's ranks.

These areas can be defined as set design, set construction, lighting, sound, costume design, costume construction and properties.

Set design, of course, requires someone who has artistic talents, but who also has an interest in the theatre, who is prepared to discuss and adapt his ideas to stage requirements and if possible, someone who has a rudimentary knowledge of construction. This is asking a great deal, which is probably why set designers are difficult to find, but the difference that a well-designed set can make to a play is enormous. In attracting a set designer, it should also be emphasised that they will, in all probability, have to do most of the actual painting themselves although willing helpers will usually be found to apply the base colours.

Actually, there are more artists about than might be imagined. Art teachers at local schools, freelance design artists, employees of advertising agencies and members of art clubs are some which spring to mind, and at perhaps one stage removed, towns which have a further education centre all run art classes and a word with the teacher might reveal a suitable candidate. Societies should bear in mind that in appointing a set designer (or designers since there is no reason why the same person should design every show) they are appointing someone who is going to be asked to do an important creative task on their behalf. It is certainly necessary that the society should take the initiative but it is equally necessary that they should conduct their search with care so that the right individual is found.

Whereas set design definitely calls for someone who has a direct feeling for the theatre, set construction, as such, does

not, although it is always desirable that everyone concerned
with a production has an interest in the theatrical side of the
activity. Set construction, in essence, is carpentry, and varies
from the extremely basic which most do-it-yourself house-
holders can well manage, to the extremely skilled. The set
construction team can therefore be a mixture of willing husbands not afraid of cutting dozens of half joints and one or two
skilled carpenters for the more complex work. The recruitment
grounds for the carpenters are school leavers who have shown
an interest in this kind of work, technical or further education
colleges or advertisements in the local press. It is unreasonable
to expect someone coming into a society straight from school,
and probably without theatrical experience, to take important
decisions on the society's behalf. This highlights the importance
of the stage director which has already been discussed.

Finding a good lighting technician and to a lesser extent
a sound technician from scratch, presents more difficulties
than most since there is no very obvious point of conversion
from an existing hobby. Furthermore, in both these posts,
work-satisfaction will be derived from the functioning of
equipment and, unless a society is both wealthy and well-
equipped, the equipment with which these individuals will be
asked to work will be very sub-standard. Too often their function will be in making the best of a bad job and this is not a
very attractive prospect to hold out to anyone.

The task of the society seeking such members is to show
them the pleasure that can be derived from applying their
talents and interests to theatrical use and the satisfaction that
comes from a good effect ingeniously contrived on old equipment.

Some years ago I had the task of lecturing on Liberal Studies
to a set of apprentice electricians who were on day-release.
They were considerably less than enthusiastic about having to
'waste' an hour each week in this way and after some weeks
I arranged with a local theatre to take them on a short visit
backstage to see the lighting switchboard. They were all fascin-
ated and willingly prolonged the hour for as long as the theatre
staff were prepared to have them. It struck me then and has
been borne out by experience since, that among young people
genuinely interested in electrical work, was a good recruiting

ground for lighting engineers. If this method of recruitment is used, then training becomes a necessity. Generally firms marketing theatrical lighting run regular training courses to which a really enthusiastic recruit can be sent. If not, then more local, if less satisfactory methods of training can be used. In the long run learning in the hard school of experience will eventually pay off.

Sound engineers are equally hard to find, although in almost any town there are firms or parts of firms dealing with recording and amplifying equipment. Dozens of people have a genuine interest in the tape recorder in its domestic applications. Provided, again, that the society is prepared to take the initiative, someone with these talents, as well as an interest in the theatre, can usually be found. Sometimes too, firms which market tape recorders or other sound equipment will look after the sound for a show provided that suitable acknowledgement is made in the programme. The advantage of organising the sound in this way is that the firm in question will generally use its own equipment which will quite probably be better than that possessed by the society.

When discussing the function of the costume designer we are moving back to the sphere which we left when discussing set design. Here again we are back in the artistic creative field and it is fair to say that the areas of obvious recruitment for set designers are much the same here, though the field of search is wider. Many modern dress shops employ people who are possessed of artistic talents and who also have a very real interest in clothes and materials. The candidate must clearly be able to draw creatively and to have a feeling for colour; what they will probably have to learn is that they not designing for daily wear. Many materials on a stage will react well or badly under light and others which are substitutes will look more like the real thing than the real thing itself. This knowledge can be learned by trial and error. As the set designer must have some knowledge of construction, so must the costume designer, although this is not necessarily part of her job.

The function of the costume designer should not be confused with that of the wardrobe mistress, although the two functions can be, and frequently are, combined into one. The task of the costume designer is specific to a single show, the task of the wardrobe mistress is a continuing one from show to show, as the lady in charge of the society's wardrobe. There will also be many productions (such as non-costume shows) in which there will be no need for a costume designer as such but in which the wardrobe mistress will still have to ensure that each character has an adequate costume.

The wardrobe mistress will also be in charge of the various helpers who will convert the creations of the costume designers into actual garments. Probably the wardrobe mistress will buy all materials centrally and may even have the garments cut out centrally before issuing them out to be sewn. People to sew the garments are not usually difficult to find, and a great many girls find real enjoyment in sewing for the stage provided that they are not overloaded. A wise wardrobe mistress will arrange for many willing pairs of hands and very close central control.

In the context of this chapter, the word 'properties' is being used in a very wide sense. It is being used to mean, not simply ensuring that a character goes on stage carrying a book, which requires no particular talent but also includes such things as making joints of meat so that they look succulent and edible. To do this well requires flair, and, done well, it makes a great deal of difference to a production. However, there is no obvious recruiting ground for such individuals. All that can be said, a little unhelpfully, is that as the backstage team takes shape and gathers impetus, so people with these talents will, almost certainly, emerge.

Stage management

Under the stage director, the backstage team will be controlled by the stage manager. Although these two posts are frequently combined, my own experience is that it is better if they are not. After all, they have different priorities. Naturally they must work in the closest liaison, but while the stage manager is the tactician, the stage director is the strategist. It is the stage director who agrees the overall backstage policy with the committee and sees to it that it is implemented. The stage manager is concerned with the allocation of tasks and carrying them out for a given production. It is he (or she) who gives the orders on the day of performance and it is to him that the various backstage departments are responsible. The stage director, while he is clearly responsible for the initial creation of the backstage team, is primarily concerned, in relation to an individual show, with the backstage budget.

We have now discussed the personnel who together make up a backstage team. It is, perhaps, desirable to reiterate what has been said already about the importance of the sequence of events. First of all the committee must agree on a policy concerning its backstage which will be a long-term one. Then it will appoint a stage director whose overall responsibility the creation of the team will be. Next the basic facilities must be provided. Any successful recruitment will be only of a temporary nature if those recruited are required to work in cold, ill-lit conditions in the middle of a winter evening. Last of all comes recruitment which the society must initiate and which must be conducted with discrimination and considerable patience. Our discussion of the creation of a backstage team has also taken the form of outlining the ideal which, it is recognised will, in practice, be unlikely to be fully achieved. However, the extent to which a society is prepared to chase the ideal will be the measure of its acceptance of the all-important contributions made by the backstage team to the artistic success of any production.

The use of acting members

Earlier in this chapter mention was made, in passing, of the use of actors as stage hands etc. It is now necessary to expand on this point slightly. Two questions arise. Firstly, is it desirable to use actors in this way and secondly, is it reasonable to ask them to do this work?

The point has already been made that the absolutely ideal situation has a totally specialist backstage team in all its departments. It is also true that in only a very few societies will this situation obtain. Given that there is a need, it is difficult to see who, other than actors can be used although it is always better to use actors who are not in the show at all rather than place the burden on those playing small parts. Even the smallest part requires the actor's full concentration to play well and it is as well if he is not distracted from it by other responsibilities.

The cast as a whole can be used as a labour force to shift the scenery etc, from the store to theatre and can, if necessary, be asked to help in its erection or on site painting. The practice of using the cast in this way is, of course, widespread. But it should be used with discretion. The producer who permits his cast to be used regularly for backstage work during the preparation period will almost certainly incur the penalties of lateness at rehearsal and lack of concentration during rehearsal. Similarly, if the cast are used extensively in erecting the set on the day before the show, so that they go into the first performance tired, they will almost certainly give a poorer performance.

The willingness of the individual actor to take part in these 'other tasks' should largely be governed by the custom of the society. If a particular society always meets the Sunday before the production to clean the theatre and erect the set, then his acceptance of a part should be taken as indicative of his willingness to conform. Similarly, actors not in use in a production should, one feels, have sufficient loyalty to that society to lend a hand in any department, if required. No one in an amateur society should consider himself to be just an actor.

Conclusion

Enough has been written to show that the present writer holds the view that the backstage team as a whole, and the individual members of it are some of the most valuable members of any society and that their technical competence and personal enthusiasm is at least as important as that of the actor. A society which undervalues its backstage team or, worse, considers the members of it to be second class citizens, inferior in some way to its actors — and this is not unknown — will never achieve the artistic standards which only a competent and valued backstage team can ensure.

7 Doing it yourself

Desirability of being self-sufficient

Many societies always hire the sets and costumes for each show that they produce. This is certainly the easiest way of dealing with both of these requirements and, in the case of sets, may even be essential if the theatre requires 14 ft. or 18 ft. (420 cm or 520 cm)* flats which are difficult to build and even more difficult to store. For a great number of societies, however, making the equipment which they will use is both rewarding in itself and, bearing in mind the cost of hiring such items, financially desirable.

Given the existence of a backstage team, making your own sets and costumes should present no insuperable problems and can be a useful investment. If well made, these items will last for several years, and the capital cost of making them is considerably less than the cost of hiring for each production.

---

*In referring to sizes of flats, imperial measurements have, in all instances been given first with the approximate metric equivalents in brackets afterwards. This is because, at the time of writing (1977), metric conversion is not complete in the UK for timber and board supplies. A sheet of hardboard is still supplied in imperial measurements and this naturally governs the size of the resultant flat. Wood, however, has been converted and 2 in. by 1 in. battening is now, in fact, 5cm x 2.5 cm. Lengths of battening have to be ordered in metric feet (commonly known as Units) but since 2.5 cm is not exactly one inch, but very slightly less, so one metric foot (or 30 cm) is actually only 11¾ inches. To buy battening, therefore, which will fit the long side of the 10 ft. sheet of hardboard, it is necessary to buy 11 metric feet (10.77 imperial feet) and to cut about ¾ in. off one end in order to fit the hardboard.

The construction of flats

A flat is, basically, a very simple piece of carpentry and assuming that it is 10 ft (300 cm) in height (normally adequate for most amateur societies), easy to build. It consists of two upright pieces of timber 2 in. x 1 in. (5 cm x 2.5 cm) and three cross pieces, one across the top, one across the base and one across the middle for support. The timber should be joined with half-joints at the corners and strengthened there by triangular pieces of hardboard, pinned and glued into position. In assembling it, care should always be taken that the frame is exactly rectangular so that it will stand straight on stage against the flat next to it. This can best be ensured by repeatedly checking it in construction against the hardboard. When the frame has been cut and assembled with 2 x 1 in. (2.5 cm) screws at each joint, it should be covered with hardboard, making sure that the end which is designed to be the base is exactly flush. Nowadays it is often difficult to buy sheets of hardboard 4 ft x 10 ft (120 cm x 300 cm) and when they are obtainable, long storage at the timber merchants often results in a crinkling at the sides which is difficult to straighten and which will result in an uneven surface to the flat. On the whole it is better to pay slightly more and to buy two pieces of hardboard 5 ft x 4 ft (150 cm x 120 cm) for each flat, joining them across the centre support piece and covering the join with masking tape.

The hardboard should be fixed to the frame by being first glued with normal woodworking adhesive and then pinned with 1 in. (2.5 cm) nails set about 6 in. (15 cm) apart all the way along the surface. Sometimes a screw in each corner for added security is a good idea but apart from this and cleaning up untidy edges with a surform or plane, there is nothing more to do to the flat which can easily be assembled by two people in an hour. Sawn timber, which is cheaper than planed timber can be used for the flat since none of it will be visible and the rough side of the hardboard should always be fixed outwards because of light reflection. The hardboard should always be soaked overnight before it is nailed into position so as to flatten it, and soaked again before paint is applied. If the society is lucky enough to possess a member who has the skill required to stretch canvas, then a canvas flat, as opposed to a hardboard

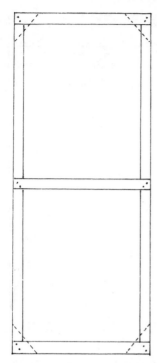

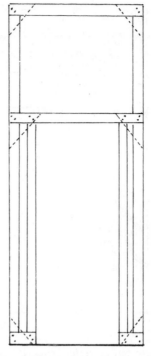

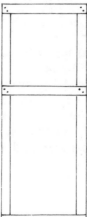

Top left: simple design for basic flat.
Top right: modification of the basic
flat to make a door flat together with
diagram of door (below).
Each corner is joined by a half joint,
secured with two screws. Across corners
(dotted) are hardboard off-cuts for
strengthening. Across base of door flat
is metal bar for stability. Note that the
cross piece on the door is not central
so that it can be used for the door
handle.
Scale: approx. 1cm = 1 foot.

How to build simple flats

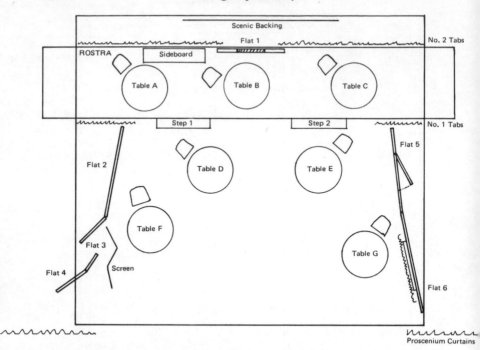

Simple but effective set design for Separate Tables *— a play which presents setting difficulties for amateurs. Most of the flats used are unchanged throughout, but can be adapted for both dining room and lounge*

one is much lighter and easier to handle. At the time of writing (1977) the total cost of building a one-sided 10 ft x 4 ft (300 cm x 120 cm) flat with hardboard is approximately £10. Assuming that the carpentry is good enough to enable it to last for — say — eight shows, then the capital cost recovery of £1.25 per flat per show is extremely reasonable.

This standard flat can be made by almost any home handiman and can be made quickly provided that two people are working together. Its construction requires little woodworking skill, as such, but it does need to be done carefully. A well-made flat will last for several years: a shoddily-made one may not last one show.

Other flats such as window flats, door flats, french windows, etc., can be regarded as variations on the basic theme although being more intricate in their design, they require more skill

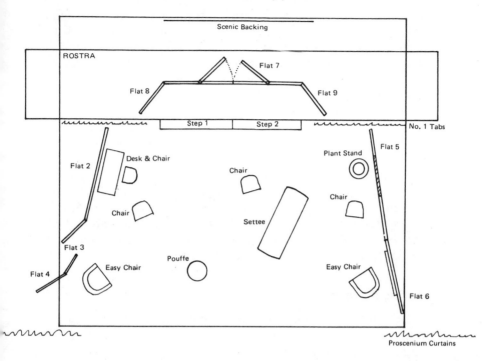

in making. As the illustrations show, it is mainly a question of increasing the wood battening to give the necessary supports and, in the case of a door flat, the essential metal bar across the base. Doors themselves and doorways need to be made with the greatest care since it is essential that they open smoothly on stage. A ball catch fastening, though the easiest, has the disadvantage of exerting pressure on the flat when it is being opened and may shake the scenery. Old door catches fastening on the stage side are usually the most satisfactory.

Although the cost of a plain flat — at 1977 prices about £10 — and of a door or window flat (£16) is reasonable when considered over the long term, it nevertheless represents an appreciable capital expenditure (perhaps £150) for most amateur dramatic societies. This highlights again the necessity for any society to have a very definite policy. The current bank balance and production profits may be inadequate to meet such expenditure and money-raising ventures may have to be organised in order to pay for the building. If this is so, then it is vital that the money so raised should be spent wisely and not with just one show in mind.

If necessary, a full set of flats need not be made at one time. Almost any combination above four can be used to set a play with the judicious use of curtains and the ingenuity of a set designer. Indeed, some of the most effective sets are ones in which flats themselves are few and ingenuity is used to the utmost. The existence of a good set designer in a society is the controlling factor on how many flats should be made for stock. It is not being argued here that societies should accept a box set as standard, simply that the construction of good lasting flats is neither particularly difficult nor demanding and is well within the competence of most small societies.

Sharing the burden

In an effort to recoup its capital expenditure on set construction, many societies endeavour to hire their flats out to other societies. This is a good idea provided that the hire charge is a realistic one. However soundly made any flat will only last a given number of shows, and each time it is taken out of store and erected on stage it will depreciate. With the advice perhaps of its auditor, a society must decide at the outset how many shows it expects a given flat to last or, rather, after how many productions its capital value will have been written off. Also, as the auditor will doubtless advise, the cost of replacing the flat after write-off must be borne in mind. Thus, if a flat costs ten pounds to build, is estimated to last six productions, and the society does three shows a year, then the flat will be written off in two years. Inflation and rising prices may mean that this same flat will cost £14 to rebuild when its two shows, or six years life is up. Therefore, its effective depreciation per show is not £1.66 (one sixth of the construction price), but £2.33 (one sixth of the replacement price). If, therefore, a society hires the flat to a kindred society, then to hire it for any sum less than about £2.50 incurs direct financial loss and the transaction can hardly be said to be worthwhile unless the charge is at least

£3.50 or £4.00. These financial details do not always occur to a committee but a good treasurer or auditor should be able to give the appropriate advice.

Again with a view to minimising the high cost of set construction it is occasionally possible for a number of societies to share flats. Desirable as this may seem on the surface, the difficulty involved in several treasurers, employing different accounting methods, agreeing on how the part-ownership will be shown on their balance sheets is likely to be considerable. None of the various difficulties involved is, of course, insuperable and the prospect of different societies working together for a common aim can only be encouraged. However, the most convenient way is probably for one society to own the flats and to hire them at cost to the others.

An interesting variation of the sharing system which I once encountered was a successful combination of the backstage teams of several societies who combined their various individual talents into a single, highly mobile, and thoroughly competent team. Their existence made a backstage team as such virtually unnecessary in about five different societies. This organisation built up its own stock of flats and backstage equipment which it then hired out, together with personnel to operate it, to the various societies which it served. The experiment was very successful but, of course, it was only possible because somewhat unusual conditions applied. These conditions were that there were a sufficient number of societies, reasonably near together, reasonably friendly, who lacked a complete backstage team of their own, and who had funds to enable them to hire one. A combination of all these conditions is comparatively rare but when it does apply, it is a useful way around the problem of understaffing backstage in small societies.

Storage

Having discussed the construction of sets, a word is necessary about the conditions in which they are made and stored. A single room doing double duty as a workshop and store is seldom satisfactory, although it may be all that is available. The tendency is always to use the room primarily as a store and the space available for workshop use becomes progressively less. Here it will be assumed that the two rooms are different.

A store is a place where you are able to find things. This sounds obvious, but it is frequently disregarded. In the one place where, above all, neatness and order should predominate, chaos usually reigns supreme. The reasons for this are not hard to find. After a show is over and the euphoria has subsided, the breaking up of a set is a mournful and depressing business which most people want to get over as soon as possible. The tendency is to hurl the equipment from the lorry into the store and to get away as soon as possible without the least thought of finding anything again. This can be prevented by the appointment of a storeman as an important member of the backstage team. His job is to issue out and recieve goods from the society's store and to insist that they are stored away logically and in places where he knows he can find them. He should also maintain a detailed inventory of all society property. If any society thinks that this is a waste of time, let them endeavour to cost the loss of and damage to their equipment and properties in the course of a year. They will probably frighten themselves.

The method of storage is also important. Items should be stored in such a way that they can be readily found and without turning the rest of the store upside down to do so. For instance, if space dictates that all flats are stored together, then the widest should go against the wall and the narrowest in front, so that all are readily visible from the front. Where possible, window and door flats should be stored separately from plain flats; again for ease of identification and access. Flats should always be stored slightly off the ground (a double row of battening is all that is necessary) and two pieces of off-cut battening should be put between them to allow the air to circulate. This way they will last longer.

It is always a good idea to build shelving; a process which is quick, cheap and easy, to accommodate smaller items such as properties and curtains, so that they will be much easier to find. Access to the store should be limited to essential users. No one is suggesting that club members are dishonest but they can be careless and it is unreasonable to expect a storeman to look after society property if all and sundry are able to enter his store at will. These precautions against loss or damage are all elementary and would be followed without question in any commercial concern.

Lighting and sound

A society's ability to achieve good results in lighting and sound depends entirely on the equipment which is available. Improvement is generally dependent on the purchase of ready-made equipment rather than cost saving do-it-yourself schemes. Occasionally, a society has funds which can be invested, and if this is the case, then the purchase of lighting and sound equipment can be worthwhile. When buying such equipment it is always sensible to obtain technical advice from the firm supplying it. They will be quite used to amateurs seeking advice in this way and, more often than not, retain a special advisory service for this purpose. Since any funds spent will be limited it is essential that what is spent, is spent in the best possible way.

Where funds will not run to the purchase of lighting equipment, it is well worthwhile inquiring if there are sources from which it can be borrowed, or hired cheaply locally. Most Town Halls, for instance, maintain a number of mobile lights suitable for stage work and which are used for special occasions. If approached, they are quite likely to be willing to lend them. An invaluable piece of equipment for any production is a dimmer board. Given very limited funds and a basic technical knowledge it is quite possible to make one. Most electricians would be able to do so with ease and the possession of this can transform a society's ability to achieve useful lighting effects with even the most basic equipment.

If a society decides to buy sound or amplification equipment for its work, it is better to wait until sufficient funds become available in order to buy really good quality. Tape recorders which are excellent in a sitting room are usually not adequate for a theatre and poor results will be obtained. Also it has to be remembered that any tape recorder will not be usable unless it is properly amplified, and the amplification equipment is therefore equally important. Here again, such equipment can sometimes be borrowed from Town Halls or similar places but it is always sensible to have it checked and adjusted by an expert before use as it may not have been well maintained.

According to a society's priorities, lighting and sound can easily constitute the most expensive area of backstage activity.

If such money is to be spent wisely it will probably have to be spent over a period, and this emphasises yet again the necessity for a society first to formulate, and then to follow a long-term policy with regard to its backstage requirements. If this is not done, then a waste of money is almost inevitable.

The wardrobe

Good wardrobe contributes to the success of a production, to quite as great an extent as good scenery and lighting. By contrast, however, to good sets, lighting and sound, good wardrobe does not necessarily have to be a highly expensive item on the balance sheet. In a modern-dressed play, of course, it will cost virtually nothing at all, but when a society does costume productions, wardrobe becomes a much larger and potentially more expensive item. In this instance, there is much to be said for making the costumes, and then of keeping them as a source of revenue.

The guiding principle for any wardrobe mistress purchasing materials for stage costumes is the effect which stage lighting and the distance between audience and actor will have upon the materials. Frequently, heavy materials will appear to best advantage; often coarser grained materials will reflect the light better. These are by no means always the most expensive and some of the cheapest materials obtainable can be the most effective. For instance, old curtain material and coarse-grained hessians look superb and have a life far in excess of many of the more expensive stuffs, however superior the latter may look at close quarters.

If a supply of period costumes is known to be wanted in the future, then it is a wise policy for the committee to supply the wardrobe mistress with a modest financial float which will enable her to stock up with material for the future costume requirements in advance. A round of the local jumble sales, purchasing old garments for the sake of the material which they contain can produce some almost unbelievable bargains. So too can close liaison with soft furnishing shops to buy up remnants of suitable colours for sometimes less than sale prices. An appeal to members too, will often achieve useful results. Many will be able to supply old sheets and if these are dyed they can form the basis of excellent costumes, all at no charge to the society. As well as stocking up with materials for future conversion into costumes, a good wardrobe mistress will have an inexhaustible supply of oddments, such as buttons, feathers, lace, braid, buckles and pieces of jewellery. If the wardrobe mistress pursues this policy intelligently and with future productions in mind, an invaluable stock will be built up at an unbelievably low cost.

A well-run wardrobe department in a society, fully staffed, will consist of four distinct sub-departments which may overlap. First there is the costume designer who, as the name implies, designs the costumes and produces colour sketches of them. Then there are the skilled dressmakers who are competent to cut out the materials and to produce rough working patterns for the seamstresses. The seamstresses themselves sew up the garments from the patterns provided and the whole operation is supervised by the wardrobe mistress who, although she may well combine it with other functions, is in this context responsible for the administrative side of the process.

Hiring out the costumes

The garments thus made will no doubt be used to good effect in the production for which they were designed but this is by no means where their useful life ends. Naturally they can be used again or adapted for future productions by the society but they can also be hired out to outside users. Nowadays the demand for costumes for fancy dress dances, pageants, other dramatic productions and the like is very considerable and for a modest charge which the public is more than willing to pay, costumes, far from being a financial drain, can become a real source of revenue.

Naturally it is much easier to run a costume hire business if all costumes are stored centrally but this is not always possible. It may be necessary to split the costumes amongst a number of private houses for storage and although this is sometimes administratively rather inconvenient, it usually works well enough if the wardrobe mistress has an efficient accounting system for them and knows exactly where each is at any one time. Whether the costumes are stored centrally or split up,

they should be graded logically. Thus if there are a number
of different historical periods, they should be stored in separate
places so that a hirer, looking perhaps for an Elizabethan
costume, can go straight to a certain rack and view all the
society's stock. Costume accessories, such as hats, belts and
tights should also be stored separately, since they can be used in
conjunction with varying costumes and may very well overlap
different historical periods.

Before leaving the subject of costume storage and costume
hire it is as well to lay emphasis on the fact that a society
attracted by the revenue accruing from hiring is placing a
heavy administrative burden on the shoulders of the wardrobe
mistress. Prospective hirers will ring her up at any time and will
usually want their requirements dealt with rapidly. Unless she
happens to store the costumes at her own house, this will mean
frequent trips to the wardrobe at all times of the day or evening.
Hirers will be very diligent about collecting the costume but
may not be so anxious to return it and this can mean chasing
them. Sometimes it is possible to make one member of the
wardrobe 'staff' solely responsible for the costume hire side of
the society's activities and this is, of course, ideal.

The only justification for accepting the burden of work that
costume hire involves is that it represents an appreciable source
of income to the society. If this is to be achieved it must be
run on a thoroughly business-like basis. Like flats, a costume
will depreciate to some extent each time it is hired out and this
depreciation should be taken into account in the hire charge.
Similarly, when a hired costume is returned it will usually need
to be cleaned, and the cost of such cleaning should be reflected
in the charge. It is always best to take the money from hirers
as they collect the costumes, issuing a receipt at the same time
in a simple duplicate book as this saves the time and trouble
of collection after the event which is always more difficult.
Some societies protect themselves against loss or damage to
their costumes on hire by insurance, but the premiums tend to
be rather high and a returnable deposit system is usually easier.
The returnable deposit system also facilitates the swift return
of the costumes if it is made clear that a certain part of the
deposit is forfeit if the costume is returned late.

All this involves a considerable amount of accounting, both

in stock control and in the financial transactions. It is clearly advisable, therefore, to consult the society's treasurer or auditor before starting hiring so that an accounting system can be imposed which is easy to control. Having taken account of all these cautions, however, there is no doubt that costume hire can represent a source of very real income to the society. If energetically handled it can not only pay for any costume requirements which the society itself may have, but also provide a very useful surplus which, at the discretion of the committee, can be invested in those other, and more expensive aspects of backstage activity which have also been the subject of this chapter.

8 Filling the seats

A society's policy towards publicity

The policy of amateur dramatic societies towards its audiences, from the point of view of quantity, varies. There are some who, frankly, are mainly interested in putting on a play for their own enjoyment and regard the audience as being almost incidental to the exercise. To these societies the necessity of filling the seats is a matter of low priority, and jumble sales or raffles are used to make up any financial deficit. Such societies, however, are few and far between and, having been mentioned, can safely be disregarded in the context of publicity.

There are other societies who are in the happy position of not having to bother about publicity unduly. These are mainly the theatre clubs, often functioning in their own theatre with limited seating capacity, and large non-acting membership. For these fortunate societies, it is merely necessary to announce a forthcoming production in a newsletter or similar membership vehicle and to invite advance bookings.

Again there are a few societies who are so well known in a given area and whose work is so highly esteemed, that the most basic and inexpensive forms of publicity are all that is required to ensure full houses. For them, too, publicity is a minor consideration. All these societies, however, constitute a very small minority of the total number. For the vast majority, publicity is a very major consideration indeed and, frequently, the most expensive single item on the budget sheet. The purpose of this chapter is to enumerate the various kinds of publicity, to discuss their relative effectiveness and to offer suggestions as to how the necessary cost can be minimised.

There are various methods by which a production is publicised and these can be listed as follows: printed publicity, newspaper advertising, newspaper editorial mention, direct mail, visual display, verbal publicity. Let us look at each in more detail.

There is hardly a society in the country which does not have some printed publicity in connection with its production. Obviously the amount of printed publicity bears a direct relationship to its effectiveness. A town in which nearly every shop window carries a hanging bill, or a display site, a poster, will clearly buy more seats than one in which the printed publicity is meagre. However, such a 'plastering' can be very expensive both in terms of money and effort expended and the return may not justify the cost.

The types of printed publicity most frequently produced are Double Crown (20 in. x 30 in.)* or Quad Crown (30 in. x 40 in.) Posters (not normally both); Hanging Cards (10 in. x 15 in.) and Handbills (A5).

Posters

Nowadays Quad Crowns are far less common than they used to be. They are considerably more expensive than Double Crowns and it is now generally considered that their impact is not in proportion. Furthermore, if bill-posting sites have to be paid for, they take up double the space and are consequently twice the price, so that most societies are unable to afford them. Societies who have to rely on the generosity of shopkeepers to

---

*Although paper sizes in the UK were converted to metric several years ago, Posters are still supplied in the old imperial sizes of Quad Crown, Double Crown, Crown and Crown Folio. This is because, although paper sizes have been converted, poster sites have not. The approximate equivalents in the metric 'A' range are all somewhat larger and would not fit the poster sites. The following table shows this.

Imperial Size	Imperial Measurements	Metric Size	Approximate conversion of metric measurements to imperial
Crown Folio	15 in. x 10 in.	A3 (420mm x 298mm)	16½ in. x 11¾ in.
Crown	20 in. x 15 in.	A2 (596mm x 420mm)	23½ in. x 16½ in.
Double Crown	30 in. x 20 in.	A1 (840mm x 596mm)	33 in. x 23½ in.
Quad Crown	40 in. x 30 in.	A0 (1192mm x 840mm)	47 in. x 33 in.

display a poster in their windows will know that whereas sympathetic shopkeepers are often prepared to display a double crown poster few are prepared to contemplate one which is double that size.

Billposting on commercially owned sites, with its high cost, very seldom warrants the cost involved. However, there are frequently about half a dozen sites in a given town which for one reason or another, are extremely good ones. It is occasionally possible to arrange with the poster company for six posters to be displayed on these sites and if so then the cost involved is almost always justified. Seldom, however is it possible to arrange this preferential treatment. Normally the poster company will accept posters and display them on such sites as happen to be free and it is seldom cost-advantageous to hand 50 or 60 Double Crowns to a poster company to distribute at will.

With the exception, then, of the purchase of a few prime sites if possible, the poster display will be primarily dependent on the generosity of shopkeepers and the energy and enthusiasm of members. As with all aspects of publicity, the display of posters will be more effective if organised. An unbalanced display will result if, at the close of a rehearsal, the publicity manager simply hands out ten posters to each member present and requests them to get them displayed. It will be infinitely more effective if he has arranged the town into a series of — say — six convenient 'walks' and at the rehearsal finds a volunteer to cover each 'walk', not only will this ensure that the whole town is evenly covered, but it also means that the publicity manager is able easily to check on whether his publicity has gone up and know who to chase if he sees that an area is not covered.

Before leaving the question of large printed publicity, the question of six-sheets should be mentioned. These are the large boards 90 in. x 40 in. (222cm x 101cm) upon which handwritten posters are pasted. Such handwritten posters are surprisingly cheap and their publicity impact is considerable. Often there is a board outside the theatre which can be used for this purpose and, sometimes, churches and other organisations own boards which they are prepared to hire out for comparatively small sums. Some enterprising societies use 8 ft. x 4 ft. flats and persuade friendly publicans to display them in their car parks. Empty shops are another excellent situation for such posters (and indeed ordinary Double Crowns) but naturally the consent of the owner or agent must first be obtained and any display that is mounted must be inside the premises. When mounting an open-air display, the planning department of the local council should be consulted so as to ensure no bye-laws are being contravened.

Hanging cards

Large display advertising, such as has been described, must always constitute the centre-point of any publicity campaign but it must be backed up by smaller printed material. Foremost among the back-up material is the hanging card or box office card as it is sometimes called. The purpose of this card is to act as a constant reminder to the public that a production is going forward and as such the frequency of its appearance is all-important. Whether it appears in the windows of private houses or in shop windows, it is essential, if it is to be at all effective, that the public sees it everywhere. To achieve this a considerable amount of leg-power on behalf of society members is necessary. Again, it is desirable that the publicity manager prepares a series of 'walks' but, because on the whole, more shopkeepers are willing to display a crown folio card than a double crown poster, the 'walks' should be shorter and more members should be involved in the distribution. It can not be sufficiently stressed that the average shopkeeper has no obligation to display your card and so, in asking him to do so, you are requesting a favour. A courteous and appreciative approach will always secure a better result.

Handbills

The other main kind of back-up publicity material is the A5 handbill and this is the item which is most subject to abuse and waste. Too often a pile of about 200 is simply left on a shop counter for anyone interested to pick up and take away. This is wasteful since, unless the site is exceptionally good, only about twenty or so will actually be taken and the rest have no publicity impact whatsoever. Small piles which can be restocked, at key points should certainly not be neglected but, as a whole, handbills should be strictly 'personalised' publicity. This of course involves the biggest amount of leg-work of all, but no one should be under the misapprehension that really effective publicity for a show can be achieved except through a considerable and sustained effort on behalf of the members.

Handbills are most effective when they are delivered by individuals to individuals. This can be achieved by parties going out and putting them through the letterboxes of all houses in selected areas. It can also be achieved by standing in the town centre on a busy Saturday morning and handing them out to passers-by. If your town or village has a station which nightly unloads large numbers of commuters it is extremely effective to have someone waiting at the barrier for them with handbills and giving them to them as they leave.

It needs to be stressed that so far, the methods of publicity suggested involve a considerable amount of manpower freely and willingly given. The publicity manager in drawing up his plans, needs to bear in mind the actual availability of such labour in real terms since, however good the planning, the publicity will still be ineffective if the plans are not carried into effect. If, therefore, the amount of available labour is known to be small, the publicity manager will do well to consider schemes which are less labour-intensive than those outlined hitherto.

Design and effectiveness

The design of the printed publicity, naturally, is all-important to its effectiveness. Here there are two vital things to be borne in mind. First, amongst all the relatively unimportant matters which printed publicity has to contain, three pieces of information — where it is, what it is and when it is — must stand out, and second, this central information (except of course in the case of handbills) must be readable from the other side of the street.

Often an artistically-minded member of the society is asked to design the publicity and, unless he or she is experienced in this particular field, the result is a very attractive picture which no one can read at any distance. Whatever sacrifices are made to typographical ugliness, publicity will have no effect unless the public can read it. Some years ago a friend of mine produced *The Lady is not for Burning*. Since he was of an artistic bent, he designed the publicity himself. The poster was a work of art. Huge red flames lapped all over it, slowly devouring Fry's heroine while other characters, beautifully drawn in silhouette, stood by. The space available for the type was so small, that much was unreadable and although the distribution of the publicity was excellent, the attendance was poor. His next production was *Tom Jones* and he had learned from his experience. The publicity was blatant, gaudy and certainly no work of art. But the house was full. Here he had chosen to throw design to the winds in order to achieve impact and was successful. Obviously, the ideal solution is a compromise, in which high artistic merit is wedded to clear legibility and impact.

Not all publicity managers are intimately conversant with the mysteries of the printing industry and much money can be spent in this area to very little effect. As a general rule it is always a good idea to strike up a good working relationship with a printer and not to be afraid of asking his advice. Nevertheless, if the publicity manager can go into the interview with some basic decisions taken, then there is clearly an advantage. Although most printers are very willing to co-operate, some are naturally better at achieving the required effect than are others. Therefore, if the publicity manager is not supplying the printer with camera ready copy, it is essential that he should see a proof to ensure that the result will give the impact required. A society will sell more tickets through its publicity by being prepared to pay very slightly more to a printer with a good reputation for display printing, than always to accept the lowest quotation as a matter of course.

As an example of the kind of decision that the publicity manager could make before seeing the printer, a second colour of ink on the publicity will usually add about 50 per cent to its cost. What the publicity manager has to ask himself is: will the added impact of a second colour sell at least half as many seats again as one colour would? If the answer is no (and it usually is) then there is no real justification for the use

The Memorial Hall, Blanktown

The Blanktown Amateur Dramatic Society

presents

𝕳𝖆𝖒𝖑𝖊𝖙

by William Shakespeare

TUESDAY to SATURDAY 26-30 JUNE

Nightly at 7.30

Admission 65p, 55p, 45p
(old age pensioners half price)

Advance Booking Office:
R. C. Smith, 41 High Street, Blanktown
Telephone: Blanktown 4732 (9-5); 3619 (evenings)

*An interesting and artistic hanging card which would be extremely diffi-cult to read from the other side of the street and (*opposite*) the same thing, inartistic, blatant and readable*

THE MEMORIAL HALL

BLANKTOWN

The Blanktown Amateur Dramatic Society

presents

HAMLET

by WILLIAM SHAKESPEARE

Tuesday - Saturday
26 - 30 JUNE 1977

NIGHTLY AT 7.30

ADMISSION 65p, 55p, 45p
(old age pensioners half price)

**Advance Booking Office: R. C. Smith, 41 High Street,
Blanktown 4732 (9-5); 3619 (evenings)**

of a second colour. The choice of the colour of ink to be used and the colour of the background though (neither of which effect the price), are important. It must be something which contrasts well and is therefore easily readable. For instance mid or dark green on a pale green background is extremely difficult to read, although aesthetically pleasing, while dark green on white reads well. Red on salmon pink is difficult; red on yellow is excellent. Whatever colour combination is chosen it is usually a good idea to stick to this combination throughout the publicity, so that its combined impact forms a unity in the minds of the public.

The method of production, too, is important if money is not to be wasted. Apart from double crown posters and six-sheets which should always be handled by a specialist printing house, the alternative methods of production are letterpress and offset litho. Some smaller printing houses will have both these processes available but an increasing number will only have litho. If this is the case, it will be necessary to provide camera ready copy which can be photographed. However it is only necessary to do this once. Camera ready copy for the hanging card, for example, can be photographically reduced for the handbill or vice versa, thus saving the charge of a second setting. If he is satisfied that you are able to do so, the printer may agree to this camera ready copy being prepared by a member of the society and further expense will thereby be saved.

Timing the distribution

Lastly, on the subject of printed publicity, timing is very important. Publicity should commence about three weeks before first night and all publicity should therefore be received at least four weeks before. The printer should be given about three weeks in which to do his work so that instructions for the publicity should be given at least two to two and a half months before performance or, in other words, as soon as the rehearsals start.

Not all printed publicity should go out at the same time. It should seek to achieve a growing impact. Firstly, three weeks in advance, the hanging cards should go up. These should be followed a week later by the big-sheet publicity and, after a

---

SPECIMEN PUBLICITY CALENDAR

Wednesday 18 April – Submit publicity specifications to printer for estimate.

Thursday 26 April – Receive written quotations from printer.

Wednesday 2 May – Production committee meeting. Submit detailed publicity budget for acceptance.

Monday 14 May – Send copy for all printed publicity material to printer.

Wednesday 16 May – Send out letters for direct mail bookings.

Tuesday 29 May – Receive all printed publicity from printer.

Saturday 2 June – Distribution of hanging cards.

Monday 4 June – Submit first press release to local newspaper before 12 noon.

Tuesday 5 June – Advance booking office opens.

Friday 8 June – First editorial mention in local newspaper. Distribute six-sheets.

Saturday 9 June – Distribution of double crown posters.

Saturday 16 June – Distribution of handbills. Dress shop window display.

Monday 19 June – Press photographer to attend rehearsal. Submit second press release to local newspaper before 12 noon. Submit copy for newspaper advertisement.

Friday 22 June – Second editorial mention in local newspaper.

Tuesday to Saturday, 26 to 30 June – Performances of show.

Specimen publicity calendar showing the timetable for the production of publicity material for a show at a given date

further week, by the handbills. Thus the public is introduced to the show, then sees it large and finally is reminded of it. It will, of course, be appreciated that the timings given above are only approximate. They must vary with the type of production, the resources of the society and the type of publicity to which the public is accustomed. It should not be forgotten, however, that there is almost as much danger in publicising a show too early as there is in publicising it too late.

Again it should be remembered that there are some shows which, however worthwhile they may be artistically, have little or no audience appeal. The publicity manager given the

thankless task of publicising one of these shows may very well
consider that some of the less direct methods of publicity to
be discussed later, are preferable to spending large sums of
money on printed publicity.

Publicity in the newspaper

The value of an advertisement in the local newspaper as a medium
of publicity is almost impossible to discuss in general terms. It
ranges from the absolutely essential to the almost valueless.
Most newspaper advertising is quite expensive in the terms of
the limited budget which applies to most shows and the publicity manager has to consider with great care the extent to
which the newspaper is actually read by his potential patrons.
Probably this form of advertising is of most value in a small
town served by a good and highly locally-orientated newspaper
which is very widely read within that district. It is perhaps of
least value in a village which only forms a very small part of
the total area covered by that newspaper.

Before leaving the matter of newspaper advertising, it is
worth commenting that its value can vary according to the play
being presented. Some plays, obviously, have a wider appeal
than others. The public is probably prepared, for instance, to
travel some distance to see a Shakespearean play, but not an
equally well-performed modern comedy. In the case of Shakespeare, therefore, there is a much stronger case for aiming at
a geographically wider public through newspaper advertising
than with some other plays.

Whatever may be said of the value of newspaper advertising,
editorial mention in the columns of a newspaper has a value
which can not be disputed. It is, after all, free. It should be
remembered, however, that the business of a local newspaper
is to report news and to print stories which will be of interest
to its readers. The story that this or that dramatic society is
presenting this or that production on such and such a date at
such and such a hall is really not a story at all and is simply
the copy for an advertisement. As such it does not warrant
inclusion. If a publicity manager expects an editor to give him
coverage, he must give him a decent story at the same time.
For instance, in a recent production of *The Ruling Class*, a

character was required to ride a one-wheeled cycle. This is hardly an everyday occurrence and his efforts to master the art provided an amusing story, a good picture and, of course, excellent publicity for the production. This, of course, is a very obvious 'story'. Others do not have to be so exotic in their nature, provided that there is a point of genuine interest in them. Good liaison with the drama reporter will be found most valuable as often, from his experience, he may be able to suggest a story line which could be interesting.

Some societies tend to be greedy about newspaper coverage and try to get something in every week for months before the production. From the standpoint of publicity, I doubt the value of this. It seems to me that two or three really good stories and particularly photographs in the weeks immediately prior to the production, when tickets are available for sale, will actually do far more good than having a series of brief mentions over a period.

Direct mail

Direct mail is another useful form of publicity provided that it is used with thought and discrimination. Its object must be to attract party bookings: to aim at individual sales through this method would certainly not justify the expense. A duplicated letter, preferably on society note-paper plus a handbill is all that is required. School, women's organisations and other groups who from time to time go out in parties are natural subjects. If a play is one with a genuine educational interest — and many are — then success with schools will naturally be the higher.

For successful direct mail selling two points are of importance and should be borne in mind. First, it is well worth while taking the trouble to find out in advance the name of the person who is likely to organise a possible party. In schools, for instance, a letter addressed to 'The Head English Teacher' or in other vague phraseology, has a way of lying around on the common room table largely unnoticed, whereas if it can be established in advance that a junior teacher, Mr Smith is very keen on outside visits, then a letter addressed personally is likely to have much more effect.

Secondly, in the wording of the letter it is important to make it easy for its recipient to make his booking. A bald announcement that the box office is open from 9 to 1 and from 2 to 5 is unlikely to be very successful since the teacher may be on duty during these hours and unable to get out. If a number that can be phoned out of working hours can be given, as well as the name to ask for, then the response will be much higher. Any form of direct mail publicity is geared to advance bookings and its effectiveness is often measured against the efficiency of the advance booking arrangements. These are discussed below.

Window displays

Of the minor and ancilliary forms of publicity, visual display — or the dressing of a local shop window to publicise the production — is perhaps the most important. Little can be said in general terms about this. Naturally it varies greatly with the play which is being presented and with the site that is available. Often there are shops in the town centre which, if politely asked, will make a part of one of their windows available to the society. After all, a well-dressed but unusual window will always make passers-by stop and they will also look at the adjacent windows.

Such windows, however, are seldom available for more than a week before production, so this form of publicity should be regarded as bringing the campaign to its climax. The usual rules apply. However attractive the display, it will be almost valueless unless 'what', 'when' and 'where' are prominently displayed and, of course, unless it can be done really well, it is better, as well as fairer to the shopkeeper, not to do it at all. Unless one of the members has a real talent for such display — and it is a specialised art — then it is usually better to allow the shop's display staff to do it for you. However, with all these reservations, it would be difficult to overestimate the impact that a really good display in the centre of the town can have.

Verbal publicity

Lastly we come to what is, in a sense, the most important

type of publicity of all: verbal publicity by members. Too often members of a society take the view that it is the publicity manager's 'job' to sell the tickets and that they need not concern their artistic souls with anything so sordid. The truth is that it is everyone's responsibility to sell a show to the public and the publicity manager's job is to co-ordinate the efforts. The extent to which all members talk with enthusiasm about a forthcoming production will undoubtedly be reflected in the sale of tickets. There are very few cases where a single member can not sell, personally, at least ten tickets for a production and this gives an invaluable boost to any publicity.

Sometimes it is possible to give members blocks of actual tickets to sell and sometimes not. Where it is possible, it is desirable, since it is always easier to sell something tangible like a ticket, rather than a committment. A useful compromise is to declare a date upon which tickets will be available to the public, to have the tickets themselves printed well in advance, and then to give them to members for sale a fortnight before the announced date, as pre-booking facilities for their friends. In a recent production of *Separate Tables* half the seats actually sold, were sold by this pre-booking method for a popular show which was also extremely well publicised. This is a measure of the effectiveness of the pre-booking method, if it can be arranged. It should not be forgotten, however, that it involves a great deal of somewhat unrewarding staff work. The business of issuing out blocks of seats and co-ordinating their return is complex and often frustrating. It is certainly worthwhile, but it should only be attempted if facilities are available.

Advance bookings

The objective of publicity is not only to induce the public to come to your production, but also to persuade them to book their tickets for it in advance. Hence the price which is advertised is an important selling factor. It is certainly always a good basic principle to let an audience feel that they have had good value for money but equally it is a mistake to underprice your show. Only local experience can really be a true guide here but purely mathematical considerations are seldom valuable. Simply to raise the price of your tickets each year by the amount by which cost of living has risen takes no account of the facts that all incomes have not risen at the same rate and that there is a definite point at which the public will decide that a show is too expensive, however well a rise can be justified by national factors.

In chapter 10 it is pointed out that a production should be costed to break even on the basis of the minimum number of seats being sold. If this exercise is always carefully carried out then a minimum price for seats will become apparent and this should form the basis of whatever decision is taken.

If the publicity is good, and a large number of people are induced to book their seats in advance, then an efficient and streamlined organisation must exist to cope with these advance sales. Seldom will a society be fortunate enough to have a professional box office at its disposal and will therefore have to create one specially for the production. During working hours, a shop in the town or village centre, easy of access and not too busy is the best answer here. Shopkeepers are, on the whole, reasonably receptive to suggestions that they act as a box office. After all, it brings fresh people into the shop and could therefore bring additional business. If a travel agency handles the ticket sales for you they will usually ask 10 per cent of the sales for such service. This should certainly not be resisted. Indeed it is a good idea to cost in this 10 per cent commission for your box office and thus provide a small incentive to push your tickets. Too many societies lose by being too mean and expecting busy business people to put themselves out on their behalf for nothing.

Most people wishing to book tickets in advance will do so because they wish to secure a good seat on the night. It is better, therefore, despite the obvious complications involved, to provide your box office with seating plans so that specific seats can be selected. It is also desirable to keep the box office open during the evening and it may therefore be necessary to transfer the seating plans from one address to another at the end of the working day, plus all unsold tickets, and to transfer them back the following morning. An alternative to this cumbersome process is for the day-time box office to hold the seating plan and tickets while the evening box office simply updates itself by a telephone call each evening. It should not be difficult for either box office to keep account of the precise tickets sold during a given session and to read the appropriate numbers over the telephone to their counterpart. Under this arrangement, tickets themselves remain in the day-time box office. Few people who book during the evening will want to take their tickets away with them and can easily be sent them as part of the following day's work.

Bookings by telephone can present problems. A member of the public, having telephoned a booking, and in his view secured a seat, tends to forget all about it until the night of the show when he turns up at the theatre box office expecting his tickets to be waiting for him. If he does, in fact, present himself at the box office on the night of the show, all will be well, but if he fails to collect the tickets, and no money has changed hands, the society will sustain an unnecessary financial loss. Because of this possibility, most societies find it expedient to specify that, unless the booking is taken from a distance or there is some good reason for it, all booked tickets must be collected and paid for within forty-eight hours of the telephone booking. Few people object to this and it is a reasonable security against bookings not being taken up.

Running a box office

The running of the theatre box office itself presents no particular problems provided that the person doing so is reasonably quick-witted and courteous. The point to remember is that almost everyone arrives within the last ten minutes before curtain up, expecting to buy their tickets and to find their way comfortably to their seats within that time. The person running the box office therefore, should be someone who is able to work extremely fast and who, if necessary, should be assisted by someone dealing solely with maturing advance bookings.

Strict accounting is vital at every stage in box office procedure and it is equally important that a proper appraisal is done after the show, on the basis of the box office returns, of the effectiveness of the various types of publicity. This is not as difficult as it sounds. Such publicity items as shop window displays and editorial mentions in the local newspaper

do not have to be appraised since they are free of charge any-
way and can clearly do nothing but good. Tickets sold by individual members will be self-evident as will party bookings
sold through direct mail. When these accountable figures have
been deducted from the total number of tickets sold, the
residual figure will represent the combined impact of the printed
publicity and the press advertising. This residual number of
tickets and their nett cash value less — say — 10 per cent to
account for the various forms of free publicity, should then be
compared with the cost of newspaper advertising and printed
publicity. If the cost of this publicity is in excess of the nett
residual ticket value, it is clearly time to consider a change of
approach in this expensive area.

Conclusion

Beyond this point it is not possible to go. The nature of the
change must be dependent on purely local factors which are
outside the scope of this book. The point which is being made
here is that such an analysis must be attempted if a society is
not to waste valuable funds on continuing to do the wrong
thing. It is literally horrifying to note the large number of
amateur dramatic societies (and even civic entertainments
departments who should know better) who continue, for each
show to produce exactly the same amount of publicity, just
because they have always done so, without making the least
effort to monitor the degree of its effectiveness. Few societies
indeed are so rich that they can afford to waste money on
publicity and yet there is no area of amateur dramatic activity
in which money is wasted, for the want of simple precautions,
with such gay abandon.

9 Producing the programme

The ugly duckling

Very often, the programme is the unwanted child of the production. When the set has been built and painted, the publicity distributed and the show is in the last week or so of production, someone remembers that before the opening night next Tuesday, a programme has to be produced. This latter day approach frequently means that the programme is either badly produced or so hastily thrown together that essential details are missing. Almost certainly it will fail to pay its way.

This unnecessary situation is often the fault of the structure of the dramatic society. The production of the programme is not the specific task of anyone in particular. The producer is supposed to have some sort of a hand in it; so perhaps is the general secretary of the society. Because a printer is involved, the publicity manager is often assumed to have the responsibility of putting it to bed. All these individuals have other more specific tasks in connection with a production which, because of the time factor, they will put first and an inadequate programme will result.

Sometimes, societies feeling that an overall responsibility for the programme is necessary, attach it to the duties of the publicity manager. This, of course, is an improvement on having no one at all responsible, but it is still unsatisfactory since the publicity manager's team is the most labour-intensive of the whole production. The likelihood of having people to spare, who can devote their whole energies to the production of a programme, is extremely slender.

The only really satisfactory way of producing a programme

is to have one person, or a group of people whose sole responsibility is this difficult and time-consuming job. They will start
their work very soon after rehearsals commence and it will
continue throughout the preparation period for the show.
Only in this way will it be possible to release the detailed
programme in sufficient time to enable the printer to do an
adequate job without undue hurry.

It is always worth remembering that after the final curtain
has fallen and the natural excitement of a production has subsided, the programme is all that remains as a lasting memento
of the show. Considered in this context it has a historical
significance, and is a symbol of a landmark in the society's
development. It is therefore worth producing in a way in which
it will form a useful and interesting document to read in future
years.

Different types of programme

Usually there are three types of programme which amateur
dramatic societies produce. The first is a single fold affair,
sometimes with an advertisement on the back page to offset
the costs of production and containing simply those essential
details which will enable the audience to follow the sequence
of events in the show. This type of programme is either distributed free or is sold for a nominal sum. It has very little
historical value and is generally the result of the last minute
rush, mentioned earlier, to produce something at all costs.
Its sales (if it is sold) will perhaps cover the costs of producing
it, but it will certainly not be a source of revenue to the society.

The second type of programme is the direct opposite to the
first. In this type, the historical significance is considered paramount. Such programmes are glossy, full and interesting to
read, contain few advertisements if any, and are reasonably
highly priced. Because of their high production costs, they
constitute a financial liability to the production. Only comparatively wealthy societies, or ones which have virtually guaranteed
box office returns, can afford to contemplate this type of
programme.

The third type of programme is not exactly a compromise
between the other two since it owes far more to the second

type than to the first. It is by far the most difficult type to produce and is the one in which cost factors play an important part. It is usually larger in number of pages than the second type, and contains at least 50 per cent advertisements. Its object is to present something which is visually acceptable and therefore historically important, while at the same time being financially profitable. Only with this third type does the programme make a measurable financial contribution to the costs of production.

Which type of programme the society produces is dependent on that society's policy; its historical consciousness; its financial needs and its manpower resources. Since these differ so widely from society to society it is not possible to enter into a discussion upon the relative merits of the different types. The first two types, indeed, require very little further comment. Most societies, however ill-organised, can find time to write out a cast list and scene synopsis and hand the same to the printer in time for him to deliver it. The second type of programme presupposes that in a society which produces it, there are members who possess the necessary artistic and editorial talents to make its production possible. A society which contains such members has only to decide whether it can financially afford to allow them to indulge their talents: a society which does not possess them would be ill-advised to try.

The programme with advertisements

This leaves the field clear for a discussion on the third type of programme. It is probably fair to say that most societies who do not already do so would be pleased to make use of the programme as a financial boost to a production if they were able to do so. Much of the purpose of this chapter is to point out some of the advantages (and pitfalls) which await a society which is contemplating moving to this type of programme.

First of all, it must be stressed that if this type of programme is to be produced, then its production must be handled by a small group of people who devote their energies to that alone. Although rewarding (in all senses), the work is very time-consuming and, if done properly, will leave time for little else.

The existence of advertisers, of course, forms the basis of

this type of programme and an understanding of the advertising potential (if any) is central to its production. For instance, village dramatic societies, where commercial undertakings are few and far between have less obvious advertising potential than societies in towns. This is to some degree offset by the fact that village firms are likely to be more 'loyal' to their local amateur dramatic society and therefore the more ready to support its efforts than town firms who are probably being approached from many quarters for similar enterprises.

'Advertisement' is rather a misleading word. The essence of an advertisement is that it is a space booked by the advertiser which, through being read by the public, will increase his business by a far greater amount than the price he paid. Because of the extremely small circulation of most programmes, few societies are able to offer this as a real possibility to potential advertisers and what they are really asking is financial support for a worthwhile local enterprise. The reaction of a potential advertiser to the price being asked should also be borne in mind. For instance, a business man will not object to spending — say £30 — if he sees that there is a very real possibility of converting it into increased business worth £500, but if the possibility of increased business is virtually nil, and he is really being asked for a contribution towards the funds, he will only contemplate, usually, a much smaller sum. The smaller sum which will be acceptable will probably not be an economic amount to charge for a full page so any theatrical programme must be based on a large number of small advertisements rather than on a small number of large ones. This, of course, adds to the workload since it takes just as long to sell a quarter page as it does to sell a full page, and emphasises the point that it is a time-consuming process.

In selling the advertisements, the stakes are not entirely loaded against the society's salesman provided that he is honest and does not try to pretend that his programme has a value which, manifestly, it has not. Most shopkeepers or businessmen will receive him courteously and sympathetically and provided that the contribution asked is not too large, a successful result can often be obtained. However, the salesman must be prepared to make, on average, about five fruitless calls before he makes one successful one and so must become accustomed to constant seeming failure. Since Saturday is a very bad day on which to sell advertising and since the salesman will probably be doing it on a distinctly part-time basis, a long period of time is required in which to sell the advertisements.

Before the advertisement salesman goes on the streets, much preparatory work must, be done in a precise costing of the publication. The first part of this process is a visit to the printer for a quotation. A good printer will advise the society's representative of the most economic means of production. He will point out that the number of pages must be a multiple of four and if possible a multiple of eight. This means that eight, sixteen, twenty-four or thirty-two pages are the most economic units. Usually, provided that the same proportion of editorial to advertising is maintained, then the larger the publication the more profitable it will be to the society. Hence, a thirty-two page book will be more profitable than a twenty-four page, and so on. It is doubtful whether a programme of eight pages (four of advertising and four of editorial) will do other than cover its own cost of production.

The necessity of a policy

With the printer's estimates before them, the society must decide what size the programme will be. In reaching this decision it must be certain that it is able to sell the necessary number of advertisement pages. Although a thirty-two page may look most attractive financially, it should not be forgotten that sixteen pages at least of advertising will have to be sold and that it could be made up of sixty four quarter pages resulting from about three hundred calls!

Before societies contemplating this type of programme abandon all hope, however, let me hasten to qualify these statements. We have, of course, been talking hitherto of societies thinking of producing this type of programme for the first time. Naturally on the first such programme the labour required is infinitely greater than on a subsequent issue for a future show. Businesses who have advertised once are reasonably likely to advertise again and this cuts down the number of necessary calls for future issues very considerably. Indeed, on the assumption that most advertisers will renew on a second programme,

the labour can be utilised the second time around in expanding
the number of pages.

It will be seen that it is necessary, if this type of programme
is to be attempted, for the decision to do so to be taken by the
society as a policy decision to cover at least three of four
productions. Also it is clearly expedient that the first such
programme should be of manageable size — perhaps sixteen
pages — with a view to enlarging it with the benefit of advertising renewal to twenty-four pages on the second issue and
thirty-two pages on the third. I have been at some pains to
emphasise the difficulty and the work involved in producing
this type of programme. It is also worth emphasising that the
financial rewards for such efforts can be very great indeed.
Many societies are able to continue in existence solely as a
result of their business-like attitudes to their programmes.

Having taken the decision to produce this type of programme
and having done all the initial costings, the society should next
produce 'dummies' which should look as much like the finished product as possible. These are the point of sale material
which are shown to the prospective advertisers. In making
the dummies it is necessary to decide what editorial matter is
going where and what spaces will be made available for advertising. Many advertisers will want to choose their positions
and it is a good idea to let them do so if possible.

Timetable of production

The planning of the editorial will probably be more difficult
than most societies imagine if they are doing it for the first
time. After all, there is a lot of space to fill and there is only
a limited amount that you can relevantly write about any one
show. It is important, however, that the space is filled and
filled interestingly since this is only fair to the advertisers and
to the audience who buy it.

Liaison with the printer at all stages is important, and a timetable of production, agreed with him in advance and rigidly
adhered to, is essential. Most small printers will need at least
a clear fortnight to produce a programme of sixteen pages or
over. The editor of the programme will presumably want about
a week to assemble the material and get it into a form which

SPECIMEN CALENDAR FOR PROGRAMME PRODUCTION

Wednesday 18 April – Submit specifications to printer for estimate.

Thursday 26 April – Receive written quotations from printer.

Wednesday 2 May – Production committee. Submit figures.

Wednesday 9 May – Commence the sale of advertisements.
Make arrangements for the writing of editorial articles.

Wednesday 13 May – Deadline for receipt of editorial articles,
programme copy from producer and advertisement copy.

Friday 1 June – Start assembling and editing programme copy and
preparing for press.

Wednesday 6 June – Submit all programme copy to printer.

Thursday 21 June – Prepare invoices and envelopes for voucher copies.

Friday 22 June – Receive programmes from printer.
Post voucher copies with invoices to advertisers.

Tuesday to Saturday, 26 to 30 June – Performances of show.

Specimen calendar for the production of the programme showing the times at which the appropriate action should be taken for a show at a given date

is suitable for submission to the printer. Before he can do so the editorial material must be written, the advertisements sold and copy for them collected. These matters will take at least a month. If a further fortnight is added at the beginning for the purpose of obtaining estimates and doing the costings, it will be seen that work on the programme should commence at least as soon as rehearsals for the show start.

Conclusion

The production of a programme may be thought to be a very small part of the whole spectrum of a society's activities, and thus hardly to warrant a chapter devoted exclusively to it. This is certainly true if the programme produced is merely an enlarged cast list, but an increasing number of societies are discovering that provided they make the necessary effort, the financial returns are very attractive indeed. It is by no means unusual for a society to make £100 profit on its programme and such an amount can make the difference between life and death to many small societies.

10 Making the books balance

Accounting methods

So much has been written in this book about the desirable ways in which money can be spent, that it is appropriate that the last chapter should be devoted to an examination of the methods of accounting that a society can employ and the ways in which a surplus can be created.

The desired surplus can only accrue from profits made on productions or through various money raising schemes in which members of the society take part. It should not be forgotten that sometimes the creation of a financial surplus is not part of a society's policy. A society may feel that provided it simply pays its way and engenders sufficient money to enable it to put on the kind of show that it enjoys doing, that is sufficient in itself. Such societies, which lack a financial surplus policy, can often find themselves in a difficult position when costs of production inevitably rise as the years go by, and the price which the public will pay for seats does not rise in proportion. As many societies have found, it is this narrowing gap between costs and income — inherent in an inflationary society — which constitutes their main financial problem. In consequence many societies who have hitherto been content just to break even are now forced to think in terms of broadening their financial policy as a hedge against inflation.

All societies have two sources of expenditure. They have to spend money on actually running the society; in keeping members informed of what is going on, paying for telephone calls and postage. All these costs are showing a distressing tendency to rise but are essential, simply to keep the wheels of the society moving. Such expenditure will, for the purposes of convenience, be referred to as the 'general account'. Then, money has to be spent on paying the bills accruing from a given production which, together with the income appropriate to a show, will be referred to as the 'production account'. Sometimes productions make a surplus which can be either banked or used for purposes indicated elsewhere which can make future productions easier.

The general account

By far the easier way to deal with is the general account. Given that a society knows what kind of communication with its members it will seek to achieve during a given year, and allowing for rising costs, it should not be difficult to estimate fairly exactly the amount on administration which will be spent from one annual general meeting to another. Since the membership figures of a society either remain reasonably constant, or show a predictable growing or diminishing tendency, it should normally be possible to arrange the subscription at such a level that receipts from this item alone will cover the costs of administration. Most societies take the view that their subscription should be kept as low as is possible so it is not to be expected that the general account will show more than a marginal surplus over costs. If it does then the surplus can be used to offset inflationary tendencies in the year following and so keep the subscription stable. In other words, the general account should be self-supporting and should simply aim at covering the costs of administration.

The production account

It seems perhaps a little trite to say that the first requirement for a society to show a profit in its productions is for it to make up its mind that it wishes to do so. In any production there are always peripheral expenses, such as the hire of ancillary lighting equipment or wigs, which can be dispensed with if necessary but which, if used, contribute greatly to the artistic excellence of the production. Hence, to take the narrow financial view of a production in which everything not specifically essential is automatically done without, may well ensure a good financial result. but may so prejudice the artistic standard, that it will react unfavourably upon future shows and the potential box-office for them. The committee has to make an intelligent and unslanted evaluation of the extent to which it is willing to sacrifice artistic effect to achieve financial success. A compromise solution nearly always results.

The role of the treasurer personalises the comments made in the last paragraph. When financial matters are under review, it is, quite rightly, to his guidance and opinions that the committee will look. It is therefore necessary that the treasurer himself should have the ability to balance artistic against financial requirements and to advise the committee properly. In many societies, treasurers are almost co-opted to the committee because of their financial expertise. Bank managers and accountants are natural candidates for this kind of co-option. Although hundreds of such treasurers, up and down the country, are undoubtedly an ornament to the office that they fill, there is, by definition, a tendency for them to take a narrow financial view of affairs which can result in a wealthy society producing second-rate plays. Accounts for a dramatic society are not generally difficult to keep, particularly if the society has a good auditor, and the treasurer ought to be as enthusiastic as the producer to make the show an artistic success, while tempering that enthusiasm with financial prudence and expertise.

So, how does our hypothetical artistically-enthused treasurer approach his seemingly contradictory job? First of all he will be diligent in maintaining very detailed records of all the financial minutiae of a production for future use and comparison. He will look very carefully at the expenditure on publicity and the results achieved by that publicity in relation to seats sold. It has already been suggested that the publicity manager will also carry out this analysis but it is just as important that the treasurer should do so. The treasurer will also scrutinise the various normal expenditures on any shows, take the trouble to check possible price increases several months in advance of requirement and, between shows make enquiries about alternative methods of supply at less cost. Such research will mean that when the time comes for him to advise the committee on the expenditure for a current production, he will be able to advise them of ways in which wastage can be avoided. This will enable him to give his colleagues who are most directly responsible for the artistic side of the production much more scope than would otherwise be possible.

The main items of expenditure in connection with a production and the fitting of a budget to the requirement has been dealt with in discussing the preparation of a production. It is certainly part of a treasurer's job to satisfy himself that estimates are realistic ones and to match them against the box office return which will be required if the kind of profit which the committee desires, is likely to be made.

When the number of seats required has been established, then records from past productions which are comparable will establish whether it is a reasonable assumption that this number of tickets can actually be sold. If this is the case, all well and good, but more often than not, the likelihood of selling enough tickets to meet the ideal expenditure, is small. Then the process has to be reversed and the number of tickets likely to be sold assessed and the individual items in the expenditure budget cut to match it. This is usually a harrowing process, since it almost invariably entails economies in the artistic side of a production which will not be welcomed, but it is essential that it is done. Such analyses are only valuable if they are accurate, and they will only be accurate if proper records are maintained of previous shows which can subsequently be used as bases of comparison. It is not uncommon for a treasurer to maintain such records of shows which take place during the time of his treasurership. It is far less common for him to be possessed of and to understand the similar records of his predecessors. This underlines yet again, that success, whether it be artistic or financial, can only be achieved as a result of a long-term policy by the society reached after great thought and employed over many years.

Other means of income

If, despite all its efforts to economise on its projected expenditure, a show still seems likely to make a loss, and profits are required for capital expenditure, the society may consider methods other than box office receipts as sources of income.

The previous chapter has dealt with the income which can be derived from a thoughtful use of the programme and there are other sources of revenue as well. Most theatres have a theatre bar which is extensively used both before the show, during the interval and after the show. Many societies perform in halls which have no bar facilities of any kind. If a bar can be arranged, it can be a very good source of income to a society. A licensee will have to apply for the licence on your behalf, and of course this can only be done if it is permissable under the hiring arrangements to run a bar on the premises. Unless the society has extensive and experienced manpower resources, it is generally better to allow the licensee to run the bar for you on a concessionary basis, arranging to share net profits with him. This means that the bar will be professionally run which is important, since waste and inexperienced handling can very soon say good-bye to potential profits. It is also important that the bar is well appointed and attractive. This is something which the professional barman will hardly have time to do, and which members of the society could undertake. The profits from the bar will be much greater if the public feels the place is inviting.

Making tea or coffee for sale is not quite as profitable as bar work but is worthwhile if the demand justifies it. This is obviously something which society members can do themselves without any professional supervision. So also is the provision of more extensive refreshments such as bar snacks or even full scale cold suppers, if the type of show (Old Time Music Hall for example) is appropriate. This can be very profitable but it is essential to sell a supper ticket with the show ticket so that those doing the catering know exactly the number on any given evening. This enables a specific amount of food to be ordered and wastage, which is such a large factor when catering for an unknown quantity is virtually eliminated.

It hardly falls within the scope of this book to discuss the various means of fund raising which are as open to the local football club as to the dramatic society. Naturally, a society can run a Christmas Draw; a Jumble Sale, a Fund-Raising Dance, or even a weekly Tombola if it has the facilities. Personally I have never been particularly keen on these types of fund-raising events, feeling that an amateur dramatic society can usually balance its books through methods which are open only to them, and that expenses incurred in a production ought normally to be met from sources of revenue directly associated with that production. If Jumble Sales or Christmas Draws are run, then they ought to be run with a view to providing specific sums (or targets) for items of capital expenditure. People will buy tickets for a draw, for example, more readily, if they know that all profits will be spent in providing two much-needed new spotlights, rather than if they are told that the money is needed to underwrite the losses on a recent production. The lesson surely, is that each show, or perhaps more accurately each series of shows should be so costed as to at least cover their expenses and, if possible to make a profit. However unpleasant it may be, societies and producers should learn to cut their coats according to their cloth both in the initial selection of the play and in the method of mounting it. After all, if the society fails to pay its bills it will go out of existence, and then there will be no drama for anyone.

Theatrical atmosphere

An aspect of financial importance which sometimes is neglected by societies, is the creation of a theatrical atmosphere. Many societies perform in church halls which, although admirable for the purposes for which they were built look nothing like theatres. There is no doubt at all that a theatrical atmosphere if it can be created, can have a cash value in the shape of increased box-office returns, quite apart from making them more interesting places in which to act. In the creation of a theatrical atmosphere, the foyer should not be neglected. It is the audience's first sight of the theatre and should reflect the theatrical mood of the evening. A few carefully hung drapes and displays of photographs to conceal concrete walls will work wonders with the atmosphere at no cost and practically no labour. In the auditorium, I have seen wonders achieved by a certain amount of carpentering skill in the construction of a removable rake over the usual floor. Displays of prints or of old posters on the walls, flower arrangements, even exhibitions for charity, can transform an uninteresting hall without any expense and very little effort. Again, of course, this is a long term policy. Patrons will have to come to two or three shows before they really appreciate what you have done, but after that it will be well worth the minimal effort involved.

Necessity of detailed records

In making these comments on finance, it has been difficult to avoid a certain vagueness. Not only do individual costs of different productions in different venues, with different limiting factors, vary so much as to make generalisations impossible, but the ability of a show to pay, or to make profits, will depend, as has been pointed out more than once, upon an individual society's policy towards finance. What can be said is that any show is much more likely to be profitable if a proper analysis is done of each departmental cost after the production and if such records are kept in such a way that they can be referred to and understood by future treasurers. There is nothing to be ashamed of in making a large profit on a production and the existence of the surplus, if wisely spent, will make possible innumerable opportunities.

On the night of a production, it is a standing temptation for all monies to be paid into a central account in such a way that it is almost impossible to separate and analyse them. This should be resisted. If there are a number of different sources of revenue — such as tickets sales (both advance and on the door), bar, refreshments, programmes, then it is important that they should all be kept separate so that their individual profitability or otherwise can be assessed and individually appraised with a view to improvement in the future, or even discontinuation. The head of each department handling money on the night should be individually responsible to the treasurer for showing separate stock and remainder figures as well as actual cash.

Conclusion

Far too many societies pay either too much or too little attention to finance. Perhaps the most difficult thing about it is to get it into proportion. An amateur dramatic society should not be run exactly as a commercial concern whose object, presumably, is to make as much money as possible. Nor should it take the attitude that as an artistic organisation, money is something rather 'dirty' with which it does not want to soil its hands. It is always desirable to make a profit on a production, provided that a proper use for the money is found, but the making of this money should never be considered as an end in itself. Curiously, societies which are most successful at making money and are lucky enough to have ready made audiences or some other factor which ensures a profit at virtually every show, tend on the whole to be over-conscious of the need for holding massive reserves on deposit accounts, and seldom spend unless they are forced to do so. In this case the money raised is sterile. Only by having a policy, which has been agreed upon after great thought — a policy which directly relates the financial aspect of productions to the artistic side, as well as to the long term aims of the society — will money raised be spent properly and in the real interests of amateur drama.

Index

Index